The Arts
Gateway to a Fulfilling Life and Cultural Age

Also by D. Paul Schafer from Rock's Mills Press

The Age of Culture (2014)

The Secrets of Culture (2015)

Celebrating Canadian Creativity (2016)

Will This Be Canada's Century? (2018)

The Cultural Personality (2018)

The True North: How Canadian Creativity Changed the World (2019)

The Arts

Gateway to a Fulfilling Life and Cultural Age

D. Paul Schafer

Rock's Mills Press
Oakville, Ontario
2020

Published by
Rock's Mills Press
www.rocksmillspress.com

For information, contact Rock's Mills Press at
customer.service@rocksmillspress.com.

Dedication

Dedicated to artists and arts organizations for bringing so much beauty, happiness, creativity, and spirituality into the world

Contents

Preface

This is a book about the powerful role the arts can play in the world as the gateway to living a fulfilling life and entering a cultural age. I have written this book because I believe that only by moving through that gateway can humanity come to grips with the world's most devastating and life-threatening problems, as well as create more peace, harmony, happiness, and equality in the world.

There are many signs on the global horizon to confirm that things are moving in a favourable direction in this regard, despite current challenges and setbacks. Millions of people all over the world are flocking to the arts to help them cope with various illnesses and diseases, come to grips with old age and the final years of life, deal with the consequences of the COVID-19 pandemic and racial conflicts, and overcome anxiety, apprehension, and depression brought on by lack of human contact, job losses, and uncertainties about the future. Just as people are looking to science to find a cure for the deadly coronavirus, so they are looking to the arts, artists, and arts organizations to create the programs and possibilities that are required to assist them in overcoming social isolation, the loss of family members and close friends, and to find the creativity that is necessary to create new employment opportunities and career directions.

As all these things happen, a new era is opening up for the arts around the world. In this new era, the arts will soar to new heights, broadening and deepening our collective knowledge and understanding of culture and all the diverse cultures and civilizations in the world, allowing us to realize higher goals, objectives, and ideals for humanity, and yielding more caring, sharing, compassion, and cooperation in the world. In this book, I have attempted to shed light on this matter by weaving together a number of articles I have written on the arts over the last few years, updating them in terms of present developments and future needs. I have organized them so that the book commences with an examination of the arts as the foundation for life, and ends by considering why a cultural age is so essential, what it is designed to accomplish, and how it can be achieved.

I would like to express my gratitude to Herman Greene, John Hobday, Alexander Schieffer, Diane Dodd, Grant Hall, Biserka Cvjetičanin, Ashfaq Ishaq, John Cimino, Susan Magsamen, Joyce Zeman, Pat Bovey, Teresa Eca, George Simons, Milton Carman, and many others for all the help and support they have provided in this matter. I am especially grateful to Galyna Shevchenko at Volodymyr Dahl East Ukrainian University for the valuable role she has played in publishing a number of these articles (as documented at the end of this book), as well as to my wife Nancy and daughters Charlene and Susan for providing constant companionship and encouragement during the research and writing stages of this book. Most of all, I am deeply indebted to David Stover, president of Rock's Mills Press, for publishing this book and several others I have written on the arts, culture, cultures, and a cultural age over the last few years. Words will never covey how much I value and appreciate his friendship, publishing and editing expertise, contributions, and help with this book and many others.

D. PAUL SCHAFER
Markham, Canada
2020

The Arts
Gateway to a Fulfilling Life and Cultural Age

Chapter 1
Foundations for Life

The best thing my parents did for me when I was young was give me an education in the arts. I have been reaping the benefits of this all my life.

Awareness of this fact has not suddenly vaulted into my consciousness. It has always been there, progressively broadening and deepening over the years as I have come to understand my good fortune and how much this has helped me in life.

My parents were not well-to-do. Nor were they well-educated. They came from farming stock—my mother from Manitoba and my father from Saskatchewan—and were forced to leave school rather early to earn a living and help support their parents. Nevertheless, my mother did manage to go to normal school and teach for several years before she got married, although my father was forced to leave school in grade ten despite the fact that he had done very well in school up to that time.

Both my parents understood the value of an education in the arts, much as many parents do. It is not coincidental that most parents want music lessons, singing lessons, dance lessons, or art classes for their children, even if they have been deprived of such opportunities themselves. They understand the value of the arts for happiness, fulfillment, and well-being in life.

My parents certainly did. I don't know where this came from, but it was definitely there. Perhaps it was because they came from European stock and were able to benefit from the high priority Europeans generally place on the arts. Perhaps it was because they saw people around them whose children had benefitted from an education in the arts and wanted their children to benefit from such an education as well. Or perhaps it was because they taught themselves to play musical instruments and paint pictures and wanted this for their children.

My mother taught herself to play the piano and the violin, and played in a dance band and community orchestra for a number of years when she was young, despite the fact that she didn't have any lessons on either instrument. My father also taught himself to play the piano—although not as well as my mother—and would often sit down at the piano after dinner and play the first movement of Beethoven's *Moonlight Sonata,* Debussy's *Clair de Lune*—or as Victor Borge called it, *Clear the Saloon*—and the first page or two of Chopin's *Etude, Op. 10, No. 3 (Tristesse)* before it got too difficult. He taught himself to paint pictures as well and produced many beautiful pastel and water colour paintings without the benefit of any lessons. He also cultivated a keen interest in classical music later in life, although he didn't have any opportunities to listen to classical music when he was young.

It is not surprising, then, that my parents wanted their children to have an excellent education in the arts—the kind of education that was deeper, richer, and broader than the one provided by elementary and secondary schools at that time and perhaps even today. They commenced their quest to do this by arranging art classes at the Art Gallery of Toronto, now the Art Gallery of Ontario, for my brother Murray and myself. These classes took place every Saturday morning when Murray was eleven or twelve and I was seven or eight. I recall taking classes from someone called A. Y. Jackson and another person called Arthur Lismer. What I didn't know at the time was that these two individuals were not just talented teachers, but distinguished members of Canada's Group of Seven, undoubtedly the most famous group of artists Canada has ever produced.

I enjoyed the classes at the Art Gallery very much. I also enjoyed all the paintings on display there, as well as the many rooms in which they were displayed. Since authorities at the Gallery were anxious to emulate European masters, styles, tastes, and techniques, most of the paintings were by artists such as Gainsborough, Constable, Turner, Goya, Vermeer, Van Dyck, and others. I even recall a painting by Rembrandt, and one or two by French Impressionists. These paintings had a lasting effect on me because they exposed me to some of the finest paintings and painters in the world, despite the fact that they were European in origin and there were few if any paintings by Canadian artists that I can remember.

Taking lessons at the Art Gallery of Toronto and seeing the many beautiful paintings there was not the only experience I had that had a lasting effect on me at that time. I also remember being asked by a little old lady on Dundas Avenue to light her stove for her every Saturday morning on our way to the Art Gallery because she was Jewish and was not allowed to light her stove on her Sabbath. While this seems trivial or insignificant, it had a profound effect on me because it exposed me to a person who had different religious beliefs and cultural customs than I did. When I look back on it now, I can see that it was experiences like this that were instrumental in inculcating in me a strong desire to learn much more about the many different cultures and religions in the world at a very early age.

It was about this time that my mother enrolled me in the choir at Grace Church on-the-Hill. *This was one of the most important experiences—if not **the** most important—in my life*. It filled me with an appreciation for music in general—

and religious music in particular—that has grown steadily over the years and endured to this day. Whenever I am bored or depressed, I usually end up realizing it is because I am not listening to enough music to keep my spirits high. I enjoy music of all types, styles, genres, and parts of the world today: popular and classical; sacred and secular; ancient, medieval, and modern; and African, Asian, South American, Middle Eastern, North American, and European. However, I am sure that it was my early exposure to "religious music" that made all this possible.

One of the best things about Grace Church on-the-Hill was all the music there was in the morning and evening services, which is true for most Anglican churches. Not only was much of the liturgy sung rather than spoken, but also there were many beautiful hymns and anthems to sing. I enjoyed singing these hymns and anthems very much, although I did not have a good singing voice. The organist and choir master at the church told me it was because the doctor cut too deep when he removed my tonsils. I don't know how much truth there is in this, but my voice did become a good singing voice—momentarily—just before it changed. Unfortunately, it was not long enough for the choir master to take advantage of it as far as any solos or separate parts were concerned. Nevertheless, I count the experience I had in the choir and the church among the richest and most valuable I have had in life.

There were many other reasons for enjoying the choir. One was singing *The Messiah* every Christmas at Massey Hall in Toronto when I was young, although we were so far up in the second balcony that it was virtually impossible to see the conductor, Sir Ernest Macmillan, who was one of Canada's most outstanding musicians and conductors at that time. Another was singing at weddings at Bishop Strachan School across the street from Grace Church on-the-Hill. Like the services at the Church, this involved singing a great deal of exquisite music and being paid handsomely for the privilege of doing so.

Yet another was going to choir camp every summer. The best thing about this—quite apart from getting out of Toronto and the heat of the city for two weeks in July or August—was being in nature and enjoying everything nature had to offer. Since the camp was held in a different location each year, this provided an excellent opportunity to get acquainted with a great deal of beautiful scenery in Muskoka and other areas north of Toronto, as well as to enjoy many pristine lakes and rivers, take long walks in the country and the forest, learn how to paddle a canoe, and eat freshly-grilled fish for breakfast most mornings.

There were pranks, too, as there are in all choirs. They occurred often, but not without devastating consequences in some cases. The best example of this was the time the Rector caught me playing a boogie bass my brother Murray had taught me on the organ at Grace Church on-the-Hill before choir practice one afternoon. I was so anxious to hear what a boogie bass would sound like on the organ that I failed to realize that the sound would reverberate throughout the Church as well as the entire area around the Church, which was located in Forest Hill, one of Toronto's most fashionable and up-scale districts. Although I thought I was alone in the Church at that time, it turned out that the Rector was working in his office that day. As soon as he heard the organ, he came flying across the chancel to put a stop to it. He came so fast, in fact, that he didn't even stop to bow to the cross at the centre of the chancel. It was the first and only time I ever saw him do this during the six or seven years I was in the choir. Did I get it that day! I got severely reprimanded by the organist and choir master following the tongue-lashing I received from the rector.

While the experience I had in Grace Church on-the-Hill choir was one of the most memorable and valuable experiences I have ever had in life, listening to classical music with my father was another. We would lie on the couch in the living room together listening to classical music on the old '78's for what seems like hours on end. The records had to be changed frequently in those days because each record played for only two or three minutes before it had to be changed. Unfortunately, this was before the days of automation, when it was possible to stack many records on the record player and play them simultaneously without having to change them one by one.

My father loved the music of Brahms, Beethoven, Schubert, Rachmaninoff, and Chopin, and instilled this love in me. He was especially fond of Schumann, who he said had a remarkable capacity for creating musical problems for himself and then extricating himself from these problems with great beauty, grace, imagination, and ingenuity.

There were piano lessons, too, paid for in carefully calculated monthly installments by my parents. Unfortunately, I couldn't play the piano any better than I sang. My piano teacher said it was because I had short fingers and a "lazy left hand." This irked me immensely because I was—and still am—left-handed, and one of the most outstanding pianists in the world at that time was Arthur Rubinstein, who had the shortest fingers I have ever seen. Nevertheless, I did manage to pass the Grade VIII piano exam and Grade II theory exam at the Royal Conservatory of Music in Toronto. As it turned out, the most memorable experience I ever had with the piano was being paid in peanuts to practice. This was recorded on a blackboard in the kitchen.

One day I remember my mother giving me nine-and-a-half peanuts for practicing four-and-three-quarters minutes. I was much more interested in playing ball hockey on the street.

These are not the only experiences I had in the arts that my parents arranged for me when I was young. My mother also read to Murray and me for what seemed like hours on end when we were young, much like many parents do for their children. Murray and I would lie spell-bound on the bunk beds my father built for us listening to stories like *Alibaba and the Forty Thieves, Aladdin's Wonderful Lamp, Tales of the Arabian Nights, The Seven Voyages of Sinbad the Sailor, Peter Pan, Tom Thumb, The Scarlet Pimpernel,* and many others. I think the name of the red-covered books these stories were in was *Journeys Through Bookland.* They were compiled by Charles H. Sylvester and were part of a universal anthology that was put together especially for children with some of the finest literary masterpieces in the world in them.

These masterpieces ran the gamut of possibilities. There were short stories, long stories, epic tales, everyday adventures, poems, and virtually everything else. They were drawn from every part of the world—western, eastern, northern, and southern—and, like the experience I had with the Jewish lady, filled me with a keen desire to learn more about the diverse cultures, traditions, customs, and countries of the world. They also instilled in me an appreciation for great literature that has persisted to this day. It is difficult to see how a comprehensive education in the arts can be achieved without this.

My parents also saw to it that I was able to enjoy a number of theatrical performances when I was young. One of the most memorable of these was a performance by an Indigenous group on the Six Nations Reserve near Brantford, Ontario one crisp evening in late September. I can't remember the subject matter of this performance, but it had a profound effect on me. Perhaps it was about Hiawatha, the legendary chief of the Onondaga tribe who founded the Iroquois Confederacy and was immortalized by Henry Longfellow in a famous poem called *The Song of Hiawatha*. But much more likely it was about Joseph Brant, the brilliant Mohawk leader and political strategist, who was friendly with the British and led the colonial Loyalists and Indigenous people against the American troops during the American Revolutionary War.

After this war, Brant settled in Ontario and became a prominent advocate and tireless negotiator for the Six Nations. He also built a farm and homestead on a large tract of land given to him in the Burlington-Brantford area by John Graves Simcoe, Governor of Ontario at that time. He became so well respected that the City of Brantford and Brant County are named after him. But what stands out most clearly in my mind is the incredible setting that was selected for this performance. It took place on and around a small lake after dark. The site was lit with huge torches, with the audience seated on the shore of the lake. It was a fascinating experience, which kept me in a state of suspense and rapture during the entire production.

There is one final area that deserves to be mentioned here because it is so fundamentally related to the education I had in the arts when I was young. It has to do with the home my parents created for us. Although this was not as specific or concrete as taking piano lessons, art lessons, singing in a choir, listening to classical music, being exposed to a great deal of marvellous literature, or seeing some enticing theatrical productions, it seemed to incorporate everything my parents knew about the arts rolled into one.

We have all been in enough family abodes to know that there is a huge difference between a "*house*" and a "*home.*" A house has all the accoutrements and trappings that are required for life and living - tables, chairs, beds, sofas, lamps, pots, kettles, a refrigerator, stove, furnace, carpets, wall hangings, paintings, and so forth. Nevertheless, this doesn't make it a home. It only becomes a home when these things are arranged with consummate care, attractively displayed, cleverly presented, and a great deal of artistry and creativity goes into ensuring they serve aesthetic functions and not just practical functions.

This is seldom a matter of money. More often than not, it is a matter of taste. Many people who have a great deal of money to spend on their residences and household furnishings are not capable of making a house a home. Conversely, many people who do not have a lot of money to spend are more than capable of doing this. We have all been in family dwellings where people have had an enormous amount of money to spend on furnishings and decorations and end up creating a place that is cold, impersonal, and unattractive rather than warm, inviting, and exciting. And usually the more money they have to spend, the worse things get! Unfortunately, they lack the artistic sensibilities, aesthetic imagination, and cultural sensitivities that are needed to make a house a home.

Not so my parents. They knew exactly how to make our house a home and had an incredible knack for doing this, which I believe was intimately tied up with their awareness and appreciation of the arts. They seemed to know where everything fit, what went with what and what did not, and how to achieve the maximum effect. This was especially true for my mother. Although she had very little money to work with and had to be careful with every penny, she knew exactly how to use pictures, wall-hangings, knick-knacks, craft objects, carpets, and so forth to warm a room, create intimacy and appeal, make every room distinctive and unique, and blend all the various parts together to form a harmonious whole. Although our house was not located in the best of neighbourhoods and was semi-detached, this didn't matter to us. It had an artistic ambiance about it that was as cherished as it was rare. This made life and living for me, Murray, and my parents, much more memorable and fulfilling than it would have been otherwise.

While the education I received in the arts when I was young was provided largely by my parents, it was supplemented at the elementary and secondary schools I attended. There were the usual art and music classes - which were concerned primarily with learning how to play a musical instrument and paint pictures - as well as a number of opportunities to engage in extramural activities, such as going to a community theatrical production, joining a photography club, or participating in the school play or annual music night. This was especially true at secondary school. Indeed, it was at secondary school that my musical horizons were expanded considerably. While I had listened to a great deal of classical music and sung an enormous amount of sacred music in the choir, I had not been exposed to much music of other kinds. This changed and changed dramatically when I was in secondary school. I have been grateful for this ever since.

It was at secondary school that I was exposed to musicals for the first time, which were very popular when I was growing up in the nineteen fifties and sixties. Most of these musicals were created by American composers and lyricists, such as Richard Rodgers, Oscar Hammerstein II, Alan Jay Lerner, Frederick Loewe, and many others. Three of my favourites were *Carousel*,

Brigadoon, and *Oklahoma*, which were all performed at the secondary school I attended although I was not involved in any of these productions. But they filled me with a love for musicals in general—and American musicals in particular—that has grown steadily since that time, including *South Pacific*, *The King and I*, *My Fair Lady*, *Porgy and Bess*, and somewhat later, *The Sound of Music* and *Camelot*. These musicals, and others, have many wonderful songs in them, such as "If I Loved You" and "You'll Never Walk Alone" from *Carousel* and "Some Enchanted Evening" from *South Pacific*. I wish these and other musicals were performed more often today, as they are filled with many beautiful songs and melodies that linger in my mind and memory.

It was also at secondary school that I was exposed to a great deal of popular music for the first time and developed a keen appreciation for it. As a result, I enjoy popular music today as well as classical music, and don't make much distinction between the two. If I like a piece of music and think it is beautiful, I will listen to it regardless of what people think or whether it is popular or classical in nature.

Many popular songs were all the rage when I was in secondary school, such as "Love is a Many Splendored Thing," "Shangri-La," "Unchained Melody," "Band of Gold," "Mr. Sandman," "My Prayer," "Sh-Boom," "I Believe," "Stranger in Paradise," and "Three Coins in the Fountain." Singers and groups who were popular included Debbie Reynolds, Rosemary Clooney, Patti Page, Perry Como, Frank Sinatra, Frankie Laine, the McGuire Sisters, the Four Lads, the Four Coins, the Platters, and many others. I enjoy listening to these singers and groups whenever I hear them—which regrettably is far too seldom—as well as the music of many other singers who were popular at that time.

I am sure this is true for all people and all musical eras. Every era produces its own pop stars who are favourites, such as Elvis Presley, the Beatles, the Rolling Stones, the Bee Gees, ABBA, Bob Dylan, Ray Charles, Barbara Streisand, Madonna, Céline Dion, Beyoncé, Lady Gaga, Justin Bieber, Drake, Garth Brooks, and countless others who have been popular over the last half century or are popular today. This may have something to do with the fact that many people have romantic attractions and love affairs in school that often last a lifetime and are usually tied up with music and the arts in some way. I am always amazed at how many people end up marrying their childhood sweethearts and spending the rest of their lives together.

Although there were many other opportunities to enjoy the arts when I was in secondary school, most of the students did not have the intensive education in the arts that I did when I was young, due to the strong commitment made to this by my parents. And I was aware of something else. I was aware of how much friction there was between the arts and sports when I was in school.

This is best demonstrated by an experience I had with the French horn in secondary school. When I was in Grade XI, I decided to take music as an option. I was told that I would have to learn to play a musical instrument as a fundamental requirement of this course. So I decided to take the French horn because it had a mellow tone and sounded nice. I was also involved in a number of sports at that time, especially football and basketball. Whenever I had to take the French horn home to practice, which was often, I would leave school early on those days because I didn't want my teammates on the football or basketball team to see me carrying an awkward looking French horn case home from school for fear of being ridiculed too much. So I would slink along side streets and over back yard fences with this cumbersome French horn case, always being grateful it wasn't a tuba or a double bass. You can imagine how embarrassing it would have been for me to be seen carrying a French horn, tuba, or double bass home from school when I was the quarterback of the football team and we were well on the way to winning a T.D.I.A.A. (Toronto District Intercollegiate Athletic Association) championship.

The friction between the arts and sports was palpable when I was in secondary school. And it wasn't confined to athletes. It affected every boy and girl in the school because sports were generally deemed to be "male activities" and the arts "female activities." But the consequences were the same. It kept boys out of the arts, and girls out of sports. Fortunately, things have changed a great deal in this regard now that girls are much more involved in sports than they were in those days.

When I graduated from secondary school and went to university, my education in the arts was curtailed a great deal, although I continued to enjoy listening to music and visiting art galleries and museums whenever I had the chance to do so. However, I didn't take any formal classes in the arts because I was enrolled in a very demanding commerce and finance and later economics program and there was simply no provision for courses in the arts. As a result, I had to settle for enjoying the arts in my spare time, although they were never far from my mind. Nevertheless, I did have one experience in the arts at university that had a profound effect on me. Like many other experiences, it was in the field of music. It expanded my musical horizons significantly, largely because it exposed me to an area of music that was not well known to me but has been an integral part of my life ever since.

It happened one day when I was walking past Hart House at the University of Toronto. Suddenly I heard the most exquisite music lofting out of one of the windows at Hart House. I stood there for the longest time listening to this music because it was so beautiful and I had never heard it before. When it was over, I rushed to the music room at Hart House to find out what it was and who composed it. It turned out to be *The Four Seasons* by Antonio Vivaldi, one of the world's greatest composers of baroque music. While I had been exposed to a great deal of baroque music through composers such as Johann Sebastian Bach and George Frederick Handel during my years in the choir, I had not been exposed to much baroque music by other composers and certainly nothing by Vivaldi that I can recall.

Hearing *The Four Seasons* opened up a whole new musical world for me. It instilled in me an avid desire to listen to more music by Vivaldi—the so-called "Red Priest"—as well as other baroque composers such as Arcangelo Corelli, Alessandro Scarlatti, and Tomaso Albinoni from Italy, François Couperin and Jean Philippe Rameau from France, Henry Purcell and John Stanley from England, Georg Philipp Telemann from Germany, Domenico Scarlatti—the son of Alessandro Scarlatti—from Italy and Spain, and Dietrich Buxtehude from Denmark. This turned out to be a "real find" for me, as baroque music has played a prominent role in my life ever since. Stated simply, I love the music of baroque composers. It is so uplifting, majestic, and accessible that it never fails to move me and fill me with a great deal of joy and happiness whenever I hear it. This is confirmed by many other people. Indeed, contemporary research is revealing that baroque music has a very exhilarating and healthy effect on people because it is very regal and evocative and affects that part of the brain that produces positive feelings and emotions.

Looking back on the many different experiences I had in the arts in my youth, both inside and outside the formal educational system, makes me realize how blessed I was to be exposed to the arts when I was young, as all people are even if they have not had the good fortune to have the rich and varied education in the arts that I did. There is only one thing I would change if it was possible to do so. I would see to it that every person had a solid education in all the arts and not just some of the arts. For although I had an excellent education in the performing, exhibiting, and literary arts thanks largely to my parents, I didn't have an education in the architectural, culinary, film, horticultural, and material arts or crafts. It was only later in life that I realized what I had missed. Unfortunately, I had to wait until I was well into my thirties and had travelled a great deal before realizing how important an education in these other areas is for life and living.

All this raises a very interesting question. What is it about the arts that makes it so essential for every person to have a comprehensive education in the arts in their childhood and youth? Since there are many reasons for this, it pays to examine some of these reasons here, since the arts in general and arts education in particular provide a remarkable foundation for life.

First of all, the arts bring an enormous amount of happiness into our lives, not only when we are young, but at all stages in life. The satisfaction that comes from music, paintings, plays, literature, dance, and the like over the course of a lifetime is enormous, especially if we open our hearts, minds, souls, spirits, senses, and intellects to the arts and allow them to penetrate into the interior of our being and consciousness. Exposure to the arts in our childhood and youth is an investment that yields countless benefits throughout life. There is simply no substitute for this.

This doesn't always have to cost a great deal of money. While attending professional concerts and plays and taking singing, dance, or music lessons can be expensive, there are ample opportunities to enjoy the arts in all communities and countries that are not too expensive if we search them out. The fulfillment that comes from this over our lives is immense, which is evident on the faces of children, young people, adults, and seniors whenever we encounter them enjoying a concert, play, painting, music, dance, or some other captivating work of art.

Fortunately, this is much easier to do today than it was in the past, due largely to developments in contemporary technology. There is hardly a person in any part of the world at present who is not able to access the arts through radio, television, film, computers, iPhones, iPods, smartphones, the Internet, YouTube, Facebook, Twitter, tablets, or some other technological device owned by family, friends, schools, local groups, or people in the community. This ability to gain access to works of art of the highest calibre by virtually every artist and arts organization in the world—past and present, ancient and modern, Asian, African, South American, Caribbean, North American, European, and Middle Eastern—is an accomplishment of monumental proportions, as people everywhere in the world are discovering to their pleasure and delight.

This is enhanced many times over when people get involved in the arts in a participatory way. The ability to play a musical instrument, paint pictures, sing in a choir, perform in a theatrical production, or make craft objects can bring an incredible amount of pleasure and contentment into our lives. To actually be able to sit down and play a piece of music on the piano or the violin, draw a picture of animals, birds, landscapes, seascapes, or people, dance in city streets, participate in making a film or television program, take excellent photographs, or fashion gifts from small bits of paper or other materials is an asset of major proportions. There is simply no substitute for this or time limit on it. It can be done any time in life, as elderly people are learning in seniors' homes and retirement centres in all parts of the world today.

The arts are also valuable vehicles for developing our communication skills and abilities. They make it possible for us to speak more clearly, write more convincingly, and express our thoughts and ideas more precisely. While I have never taken a drama course, my neighbour next door tells me that the drama course her daughter took in secondary school was *the most important class* she ever took. It helped her come out of her shell, speak in public, communicate more easily with others, and develop a strong sense of identity, confidence, and self-worth.

This is enriched by the fact that the arts are ideal vehicles for expressing our feelings and emotions. It is impossible to participate in any artistic activity without learning to express our feelings and emotions in sensitive, moving, and compassionate ways, as well as connect with other people on a deeper, richer, and more fundamental level. While the arts can be provocative at times—and must be if they are to fulfill their full mandate—the feelings and emotions evoked through the arts are usually much more positive than negative. They seldom injure people, destroy things, or produce irrational or violent forms of behaviour.

Developing our communication skills and abilities and

expressing our feelings and emotions are not the only advantages to be derived from involvement in the arts and having a first-class education in the arts in our childhood and youth. The potential exists for developing many other skills and abilities as well. While some art forms tend to be more individual in character—the visual and material arts for example—others tend to be more collaborative in character. Take drama, music, and opera for example. It is impossible to put on a play, perform a symphony, or stage an opera or ballet without engaging in a great deal of cooperation and teamwork. This cooperation and teamwork extends all the way from working together on the creation of sets and props and rehearsing scenes and movements to practicing parts and putting on final performances. Through the preparation and presentation of works of art, people learn to work collectively in the realization of common causes, goals, and objectives, thereby developing collaborative skills and cooperative abilities that are in great demand today. This also requires a great deal of social interaction and human cohesion, thereby counteracting the isolation and loneliness that comes from modern technology and is such a big problem today.

There is also much to be learned from the arts about life, living, and the world around us. Not only do the arts open up vast vistas and fertile avenues for exploration and discovery, but also they provide an incredible window on the world and everything in the world. Everything is there in one form or another: the universe, nature, the natural environment, the human species, other species, countries, cultures, history, geography, time, space, place, the past, the present, the future, and virtually everything else.

Since the arts engage the mind, body, heart, soul, intellect, spirit, and senses, they provide a way of bringing together all our human faculties to create a harmonious and integrated whole. This makes us more balanced within ourselves, as well as more in tune with the world. This is why artists, arts organizations, and the arts have been in the vanguard of the movement to create "the whole person" ever since the nineteenth century when the British scholar and poet, Matthew Arnold, espoused the need for the harmonious development of all the powers that constitute human nature. Arnold was strongly opposed to the development of any one of these powers to the exclusion or detriment of the others, as well as promoting excellence, perfection, and sharing the best humanity has to offer through the arts and education or "sweetness and light" as he called it. Not bad advice for people living in a fragmented, disconnected, and disoriented world.

If the arts are the key to developing the whole person, they are also the key to developing the creative person. As such, they represent one of the best vehicles of all for helping people in general—and children and young people in particular—to respond imaginatively to the complexities of modern life and the rapidity of local, regional, national, and international events.

As I reflect back on all the experiences I had in the arts in my childhood and youth, I can see and understand why a comprehensive education in the arts is so essential for all people early in life as well as throughout life. Not only does this enable people to reap the full benefits and countless rewards that come from this over a lifetime, but also it provides the foundations that are necessary for a happy, healthy, productive, and fulfilling life.

It is for reasons such as these that every child and young person in the world should have a comprehensive education in the arts. This education should not be limited to a few art forms, but spread over many art forms. It should also include opportunities to participate actively in the arts in both the formal and informal sense. Every child and young person in the world, regardless of whether they live in Africa, Asia, South America, North America, the Caribbean, Europe, or the Middle East, should have enough opportunities to be involved in the arts that they provide the foundations for life. There is simply no better time for people to be exposed to the arts and have an excellent education in the arts than in their childhood and youth. This is where it all begins and when it counts the most.

Chapter 2
Enriching Our Lives through the Arts

The evidence is overwhelming and conclusive. If we want to live a full, fulfilling, and happy life, we must make the arts a fundamental part of it.

When the American psychologist Rollo May asked, "What if art and culture are not the frosting at all, but rather the fountainhead of human existence?" he put his finger on the crux of the matter. For the arts, like culture, are *not* frills, luxuries, or the icing on the cake, but, rather, the elixir that is needed to live contented and meaningful lives at each and every stage in the life process, from the earliest signs of life to its final days.

Our encounter with the arts begins before we are born. Regardless of where we are born in the world, we are exposed to some of the most important aspects of the arts when we are still in the womb. This is true not only for language and the language arts—among the most important art forms of all but usually taken for granted and ignored because they are so commonplace—but also for music, literature, and all the other arts. Many mothers sing to their babies and read stories to them before they see the light of day, knowing consciously or intuitively how essential the arts are for getting an excellent start in life.

When we are born, our encounter with the arts intensifies rapidly. This is especially true for the material arts or crafts, since babies and toddlers manifest a keen desire to have tactile experiences by touching, holding, and feeling everything they come into contact with, including dolls, pillows, blankets, fingers, hands, and toes. Not long after this, they begin to play with blocks and other materials. They also begin to dance, perform, and clown around, either in public or by themselves. They also experiment with paint, applying it to paper with their hands, feet, and brushes, as well as throwing it against walls or curtains to see what this will look like, much to the consternation of their parents.

This is an ideal time to capitalize on children's fascination with the arts and numerous other activities. As Fraser Mustard, a prominent Canadian educator and advocate of early childhood education, states in *The Early Years Study*, formal education should start much sooner than it does because this is when children's capacity for learning is greatest. This is why more and more educators are coming to the conclusion that the first two or three years of life are the most important of all, despite the fact that most children do not begin their formal education until later.

One person who had a consuming interest in children and especially their education in the arts was Sir Herbert Read, the British cultural scholar and author. He produced a powerful rationale for early education in the arts, as well as throughout life, in books such as *Education through Art, Culture and Education in a World Order*, and many others. He also participated in the creation of the International Society for Education through Art as an executive arm of UNESCO in 1954. One organization that has built on Read's vision in this area and carried it further is the International Child Art Foundation, created in the United States more than two decades ago. This remarkable organization and its founder Ashfaq Ishaq employ the power of art in all its diverse forms to nurture children's creativity and imbue their lives with empathy and ingenuity. A promoter and protector of children's creativity and imagination, the Foundation organizes the Arts

Olympiad and World Children's Festival, publishes *ChildArt* magazine, provides many Peace Through Art programs, and cultivates children's ability to dream as well as to experience and exude compassion.

For centuries, the arts were treated as "ends in themselves." This caused people to focus most of their time, energy, and attention on the many benefits to be derived from the arts themselves. From the visual, material, and architectural arts, for instance, there is much to be learned about mass, density, shape, texture, form, proportion, colour, and perspective; from dance, drama, and literature one learns about balance, movement, muscle control, physical coordination, tragedy, comedy, satire, and pathos; and music teaches us about sound, rhythm, melodies, harmony, counterpoint, composition, and orchestration. These qualities can be used to advantage in studying and mastering other subjects, which is why philosophers and scholars have long recognized the intimate connection between the arts, sciences, mathematics, and other disciplines.

Over the last four or five decades, there has been a tendency to focus on many other benefits of the arts and therefore to treat the arts as "means to other ends" and not only as "ends in themselves." This includes cultivating creativity, imagination, and excellence, developing a battery of skills that are useful in other areas of life, being sensitive and compassionate, generating economic opportunities, addressing important social issues, bringing people together, sharing experiences, and contributing to the creation of a better world.

Recognition of these two distinct areas of the arts results largely from the work of UNESCO and other international organizations, the involvement of many artists and arts organizations in a variety of social causes and humanitarian concerns, the advocacy of distinguished experts in the arts, culture, and creativity, such as Sir Kenneth Robinson, and recent research and major assessments of the benefits of the arts in the world. Without the ability to create, innovate, work together, think critically, respond imaginatively, deal with a host of internal and external problems, and apply what has been learned from the arts to other areas of life and other disciplines, it is clear that people will be at a considerable disadvantage in the future.

When looked at in totality, there is little in the world or in life that is not concerned with the arts in one form or another. As a result, there is an incredible amount to be learned from the arts about life, living, reality, the human condition, and the world situation at each and every stage and age in life. This explains why Rollo May felt art and culture were "the fountainhead of human existence," and Jean Cocteau believed "art is not a pastime, but a priesthood." In doing so, he stretched a point to make a point, as do many artists.

Treating the arts seriously should cause us to open up a commanding place for them throughout our lives and not just in childhood and youth. This yields many benefits, such as the development of our personalities, lives, and careers, the more effective raising of children, the enjoyment of family life, the cultivation of friendships and relationships, better performance in jobs and careers, and much more. Not only should we reach out to the arts whenever possible, but we should also allow the arts to penetrate into the interior of our being and our consciousness. There is simply no better way to explore the many different ways the arts can broaden, deepen, and enrich our lives, enhance our understanding of ourselves and others, contribute to our identity, personality development, health, and well-being, and strengthen our associations with other people, nature, and the world around us. It doesn't matter whether this happens on a part-time or full-time, casual or concentrated basis. It will still lead to transformative experiences and transcendental possibilities.

The joy and happiness the arts bring into our lives over a lifetime results from listening to exquisite music, watching superb plays, enjoying exciting opera and dance performances, looking at memorable paintings and pictures, cherishing fine craft objects, reading interesting books, savouring outstanding stories, poems, and films, and seeing majestic monuments. Surely this is what Walter Pater had in mind when he said, "Art comes to you proposing frankly to give nothing but the highest quality to your moments as they pass."

There are billions of people all over the world who enjoy artistic experiences like these as audience members, active participants, or both. While these forms of involvement in the arts are different—with diverse outcomes, implications, and consequences—they bring us an enormous amount of pleasure and satisfaction as well as help us to deal effectively with the pressures, tensions, stresses, and strains of modern life.

Fortunately, the arts can be enjoyed in reproduced and recorded form these days and not just "live." This is due to the fact that the arts are now easily accessible through radio, television, film, sound recordings, and digital and print books and magazines. In recent years, access to the arts has also been enhanced considerably through major advances in social and mass media. The joy and satisfaction that comes from exposure to the arts in these ways over a lifetime is immeasurable. As Glenn Gould, the Canadian pianist, put it, "The purpose of art is not the release of a momentary ejection of adrenaline but is, rather, the gradual lifelong construction of a state of wonder and serenity."

One of the most fascinating things about the arts is that every art form possesses some special quality or characteristic that makes it distinctive and unique. This is true not only for the performing, exhibiting, and literary arts, but for all art forms.

In the case of music, for example, that special characteristic is sound, rhythm, and melody. Composers and musicians use these qualities to create musical experiences and compositions that express their and our hopes, dreams, aspirations, ideas, and ideals, often in deep, profound, and powerful ways. This is what gives music its tremendous power and international appeal, leading some to believe that music is the highest art form. Presumably this is why Walter Pater concluded that "all art constantly aspires toward the condition of music."

Music possesses the potential to move people to the very depths of their being. We have all been so touched and moved by specific pieces of music at different times in our lives that we feel we have transcended the world and entered a very special place. In the western musical tradition alone, melody-makers such as Chopin, Schubert, Mendelssohn, the Beatles, and countless others have had a special capacity for this. Some of Chopin's most exquisite melodies occur at the very beginning of pieces, or, in a few cases, run throughout entire pieces, such as his *Étude in A Flat major, Op. 25, No. 1* (Aeolian Harp). However, others are buried deep in the middle of compositions and are only encountered later, such as the beautiful melodies in his *Fantaisie-Impromptu Op. 66, Scherzo in B flat minor,* No. 2, *Op. 31,* and *Ballade No. 1, Op. 23 in G minor.* We have to wait patiently to hear the most enthralling melodies in these pieces, something which is also true of the second movements of his first and second piano concertos. And these are only a few examples of exquisite melodies drawn from the Western musical tradition. A vast cornucopia of captivating melodies may be found in the works of composers in every culture, country, and tradition in the world.

What sound, rhythm, and melody are to music, representation, perception, perspective, and colour are to the visual arts. Painters use these elements in many different ways to produce works that express feelings, emotions, ideas, impressions, and visions that border on the sublime. An excellent example of this in the Western tradition is the work of Joseph Mallord William Turner, the renowned Romantic landscape painter. I am thinking here, for instance, of his *Morning after the Wreck, The Moselle Bridge, Coblenz, The Fighting Téméraire Tugged to Her Last Berth to be Broken Up, The Grand Canal, Venice, 1835, The Lake, Petworth: Sunset,* a *Stag Drinking*. There is a mystical and mysterious quality to all these paintings that borders on the sublime.

What representation, perception, perspective, and colour are to the visual arts and sound, rhythm, and melody are to music, simplicity is to poetry. While every art form and artist strives to express things simply—and often achieves this goal, since this is one of the keys to creating great works of art—poetry seems to be far more concerned with simplicity than any other art form, as well as manifesting this characteristic most frequently. In fact, it is probably fair to say that poetry relies more on simplicity than anything else. This is because the challenge in poetry is to express things as succinctly as possible, achieving the maximum effect with the minimum number of words.

There are many examples of this. When John Keats wrote that

"A thing of beauty is a joy forever," the line resonated strongly with many people because a powerful idea was expressed in only eight simple words. Interestingly, Robert Schumann's musical piece, *The Poet Speaks*, also achieves this end, and does so deliberately as Schumann was attempting to illustrate this particular ability of poets and poetry in this short but intriguing piece of music. It is undoubtedly one of the simplest pieces of music ever written, along with J. S. Bach's *Prelude No. 1*, which is also very simple but incredibly beautiful and powerful.

Poetry's claim to profundity and power through simplicity is also demonstrated by William Blake and his poem *Auguries of Innocence*. This poem says so much in so few words that it possesses an awesome power and profundity that is difficult to describe but easy to appreciate:

> To see a World in a Grain of Sand
> And a Heaven in a Wild Flower
> Hold Infinity in the palm of your hand
> And Eternity in an Hour.

While these four lines express powerful thoughts and ideas very simply, it took a poet of Blake's stature to put them into words and express them so succinctly. This is equally true of the next two lines of this poem, which also possess an incredible power and profundity and are equally famous for conveying an enormous amount in a few simple words:

> A Robin Red breast in a Cage
> Puts all Heaven in a Rage.

While caging robin red breast may not put "all Heaven in a

Rage" as Blake hoped, these two lines resonate strongly with millions of people concerned about freedom and the many constraints imposed on it. They also resonate strongly with people opposed to caging animals in zoos, a practice that growing numbers of people around the world condemn because of the cruelty and injustice it involves.

John Keats and William Blake are only two examples of poets who have expressed powerful ideas very simply. There are many others, such as Elizabeth Barrett Browning who wrote, "How do I love thee? / Let me count the ways," and William Shakespeare who declared, "All the world's a stage / And all the men and women merely players." Talk about saying powerful things with the utmost simplicity and minimum number of words! Countless other poets have also possessed this ability, including Robert Browning, Pierre de Ronsard, Omar Khayyam, Pablo Neruda, Federico Garcia Lorca, Rabindranath Tagore, Li Po, Wang Wei, Du Fu, Robert Frost, Jorge Luis Borges, Maya Angelou, and others.

What simplicity is to poetry, movement and physicality are to dance. Here, too, many examples abound, especially in the ballets of Tchaikovsky. His *Swan Lake* and *Sleeping Beauty* are masterpieces filled with graceful solos and elegant *pas de deux* that border on the sublime. But this is only one example among many. Countless dances are incredibly beautiful and loved for their elegance and charm, regardless of whether they are classical, popular, folk, contemporary, or ethnic in nature. This is likely why Martha Graham, the legendary American dancer and choreographer, claimed that "dance is the hidden language of the soul."

Then there is architecture, in which mass, density, form, design, matter, and texture are the key elements. Architects make use of these elements all the time—and in many different ways—to produce beautiful buildings, leading some people to refer to architecture as "frozen music"—an apt description in view of the fact that some architectural masterpieces are so exquisite and ornate that they really do look like music that has been frozen in time and space.

While the Taj Mahal in India, deemed by many to be one of the most beautiful architectural achievements in the world, is perhaps the best example of this, there are many others. Included here would undoubtedly be the Hagia Sophia and Blue Mosque in Turkey, the Jameh Mosque and the Shah Mosque in Iran, the Golden Pavilion or Kinkaku-ji in Japan, Shwedagon Pagoda in Myanmar, Angkor Wat in Cambodia, the Temple of Heaven in China, Mezquita de Cordoba in Spain, Prambanan Temple in Indonesia, and the Sydney Opera House in Australia. All these architectural marvels and masterpieces, and many others, use mass, form, matter, density, and texture to enhance their impact and appeal. This is also true of other buildings large and small. While many Gothic and Romanesque buildings achieve beauty by enclosing huge spaces and doing so in such a way that they stretch upward towards the heavens—think of the great Gothic and Romanesque cathedrals of France and England, for example—many Byzantine buildings achieve beauty by enclosing small spaces and decorating them as exquisitely as possible. The many beautiful Byzantine basilicas in Russia, Eastern Europe, and Ravenna in Italy do this and do it extremely well. By decorating the walls, ceiling, and floors with glittering tiles, frescos, inlays, and icons, these buildings are predicated on the belief that "small is beautiful" and "less is more."

Theatre, literature, opera, and film use stories as their

special quality and specific device, and do so in fascinating, informative, and illustrious ways. This is because stories communicate things that are simple and profound, mundane and momentous, timely and timeless.

Theatre and literature are superb illustrations of this. Consider the works of Shakespeare. His stories are full of keen insights into different personality types, diverse social, political, and societal situations, human triumphs and tragedies, and individual foibles and insecurities. As a result, his plays are as revered today as the day they were written. His keen insights into human nature, the human condition, life, living, and people's strengths, weaknesses, foibles, and idiosyncrasies in such plays as *Hamlet, Macbeth, Romeo and Juliet, The Tempest,* and *Twelfth Night* are remarkable. And what is true of Shakespeare and his works is also true of many other authors, including George Bernard Shaw, Molière, Charles Dickens, Jalãl ad-Din Muhammed Rŭmĭ, and countless others. What a powerful effect stories can have on our lives, regardless of who is telling them, whether they are epic tales or everyday adventures, and regardless of how they are transmitted or presented.

There are countless stories in every culture, country, and civilization in the world that ring true because they are captivating and compelling, regardless of how they are told. These stories run the gamut of possibilities, from the remote past to the immediate present. They extend, in fact, from Homer's *Iliad* and *Odyssey* to Chinua Achebe's *Things Fall Apart* and Paulo Coelho's *The Alchemist*. In the western literary tradition alone, there are countless literary masterpieces, such as Dante Alighieri's *The Divine Comedy*, Miguel de Cervantes' *Don Quixote*, Alexander Dumas' *Count of Monte Cristo*, Emily Brontë's *Wuthering Heights*, Herman Melville's *Moby-Dick*,

J.R.R. Tolkien's *The Lord of the Rings*, Harper Lee's *To Kill a Mockingbird*, Leo Tolstoy's *War and Peace*, Mark Twain's *The Adventures of Huckleberry Finn*, and J.K. Rowling's Harry Potter series. These works, and many others, expose the light and dark sides of human nature and the human condition. And what is true for the western literary tradition is also true for all other literary traditions, regardless of where they are situated in the world.

This is not only true for the literary arts, but also for films and operas. Films are a compelling way to tell stories in visual, auditory, and musical terms as well as to preserve them for posterity; examples include the film versions of *Doctor Zhivago*, *Gone with the Wind*, and the life of Mahatma Gandhi. Despite the fact that films like *Gone with the Wind* have been criticized in recent years for being racially biased and prejudiced as well as for a number of other shortcomings, these are all films that have been watched by millions of people around the world since they were first produced. This is also true for operas, especially operas by Puccini, Verdi, Wagner, Handel, Monteverdi, Cavallo, and many others.

In addition to the special qualities possessed by every art form, and all the benefits that can be derived from them, there are also many practical ways in which the arts can help us, including the development of our jobs, careers, and employment prospects.

At one time, people were trained for a single job. As a result, education and training focused largely on learning specific skills and specialized abilities. With the high rate of occupational turnover and technological change today—it is estimated that people may have ten to fifteen jobs over the course of their lives and these in very different fields—this view is changing and changing rapidly. It is now apparent that narrowly trained and highly specialized people may not be able to deal with difficult employment situations, as well as with jobs that are constantly being transformed, downsized, altered, or terminated. In consequence, far more attention is being paid these days to educating and training people who are creative—people who can respond imaginatively to whatever employment challenges and career circumstances they are confronted with because they have learned to use their mental, physical, emotional, and intellectual powers and abilities in new, original, and highly innovative ways. It is creativity—not conformity—that will enable people to find jobs, create jobs, and perform effectively in them in the future.

What is true for creativity is also true for excellence. Regardless of what occupation or profession we end up in, achieving excellence is essential.

The arts value excellence more highly than other fields because it is necessary to master artistic challenges and perform aesthetically pleasing works. No one likes to watch an inferior or mediocre artistic performance. To prevent this, it is necessary to aspire to and achieve excellence in all artistic endeavours, and this often turns out to be the key to achieving excellence in other areas of life as well. There is a reason why we often talk about "the art of science," "the art of politics," and "the art of business," since each of these fields are art forms when they are performed with excellence. Henry David Thoreau took this idea a step further when he said, "The highest condition of art is artlessness."

It is impossible to engage in the arts without learning to discipline ourselves to use our time, talents, and faculties to best advantage. This doesn't always mean discipline by an authoritarian teacher. More often than not, it means mastering tools, techniques, methods, instruments, materials, and so forth by ourselves. This helps us to develop our physical and mental capabilities to a much greater extent, as well as to realize more effective use of our hands, legs, feet, arms, eyes, ears, minds, and bodies. Small wonder educators, social workers, psychologists, and health care providers are using the arts far more frequently to help people deal with a whole set of mental, physical, emotional, and spiritual problems that require discipline to deal with effectively and overcome.

The arts also possess the potential to develop our critical faculties and sense of discrimination and taste. This enhances our ability to make better judgements and assessments concerning a wide range of issues and problems that affect our lives, families, communities, social situations, and environmental circumstances.

In addition to this, the arts also possess the ability to strengthen our perceptual and sensory abilities. This should begin with cultivating the art of seeing, which Goethe thought was the most essential sensory ability of all because it was with the eye more than any other sense organ that he learned to comprehend the world. This ability is cultivated most effectively through the visual arts, going to art galleries and museums, and the like. This enables us to develop our capacity for perception and perspective, understand foreground and background relationships, discover links and connections, and focus on details and parts.

This is merely the first step in a whole series that is needed if we are to strengthen all our sensory abilities. For the arts improve our ability to hear, smell, taste, and touch, and not only to see. These other abilities can be cultivated through music, sculpture, the culinary, material, and literary arts, and many others. While we may not be aware of it at the time, people who take craft lessons, modern or ballroom dancing, or cooking courses in their adult years are more likely to have more developed sensory abilities than people who do not engage in these activities.

The arts also have an essential role to play in bringing people, groups, communities, societies, and countries together in both real and digital ways. They do so through the ability of artists and arts organizations to create music, pictures, stories, plays, poems, platforms, networks, and so forth *that can be shared.* This does more than anything else to create strong bonds and a sense of belonging between people, regardless of whether they live in small towns, large cities, or rural areas.

A good example of this is the work of Gareth Malone, the British choral conductor, who has created many choirs in England and other parts of the world over the last three or four decades, especially in schools, communities, corporations, and for military personnel, as well as for the Invictus Games. Malone's work has attracted a great deal of attention in recent years due to the success he has had in this area and the depiction of many of his successes in a series of television programs called *The Choir*, produced by the British Broadcasting Corporation.

Most noteworthy in Malone's case are the choirs he created in England, and especially in South Oxhey, a suburb of Watford in Hertfordshire. What made this such a remarkable achievement was that South Oxhey was an economically depressed area before Malone brought the whole community together by ferreting out many people who had never sung in a choir before—or sung in public at all—and encouraging them to join the South Oxhey community choir. It culminated with highly successful performances in the Watford Coliseum, St. Albans Abbey, the Sox Fest, and many other venues. Members of the choir waxed eloquently about how frightened they were to join the choir, how persistent Malone was in getting them involved, how well trained they were for their public performances, and how exciting and enriching they found the experience. Not only did the choir do a great deal to rejuvenate South Oxhey in social and musical terms, but also it helped bring the community back from the brink of an economic disaster. This is not only true for South Oxhey. Towns, cities, and countries all over the world are benefiting from the remarkable capacity the arts, artists, and arts organizations possess to create and activate major developments like this.

There is another ability buried deep in the arts that is of crucial importance to our lives and our development—one that is probably the most important of all when the present and future are considered. It is the capacity for holism. It derives from the fact that every work of art is a whole composed of many parts. While this is most apparent in the visual arts, it is also apparent in all the other arts. For regardless of whether it is a painting, play, musical composition, poem, story, or film, every work of art is a whole made up of many parts that are woven together in specific combinations and arrangements to form something that is greater than the parts and the sum of the parts. This is because new entities are brought into existence when these wholes are created that are not present in the parts taken separately. This makes the arts ideal vehicles for seeing and understanding things in holistic terms.

By stretching across all human faculties, the arts can be used to great advantage to assist us in becoming "whole people" and "total human beings" in the best and most complete sense of these terms. This explains why artists, arts organizations, and the arts have been in the vanguard of the movement to create "the whole person" ever since Matthew Arnold emphasized the need to attend to the harmonious development of all the faculties that comprise human nature. Not only was Arnold opposed to the development of any one of these faculties to the exclusion or dominance of the others—especially when it comes to developing our personalities, characters, identities, and lives—but he was devoted to the pursuit of excellence and the necessity of the arts and arts education. Not bad advice for people living in a fragmented world and desperately searching for meaning and fulfillment in life.

This capacity of the arts to teach us about holism is not limited to ourselves and the development of our lives and personalities. It extends to the world around us, especially with respect to all the diverse cultures and civilizations in the world. This is because cultures and civilizations, like people and artistic works, are also wholes made up of many parts, albeit on a far larger scale. The problem here, of course, is that we cannot see cultures and civilizations as wholes because they are composed of too many parts and it is not possible to see the organizing principles that serve to combine all the parts together to form these wholes.

How, then, is it possible to know and understand cultures and civilizations as wholes? In order to do this, it is necessary to turn to artists and arts organizations. This is because artists and arts organizations create many of the signs, symbols, myths, legends, metaphors, stories, rituals, and the like that shed light on cultures and civilizations as wholes and total ways of life.

Artists and arts organizations are able to do this because one of their greatest assets is the ability to select parts that are symbolic of cultures and civilizations as wholes and therefore epitomize them. The old adage "a picture is worth a thousand words" is a cliché, but it speaks volumes about the ability of artists and arts organizations to convey an incredible amount about the character of cultures and civilizations as wholes that cannot be communicated as effectively in any other way, or perhaps not even communicated at all. This point was driven home with great clarity and conviction by Robert Redfield, who spent most of his life studying cultures and civilizations as wholes:

> The characterizations of the artist ... are of course not precise at all; but very much of the whole is communicated to us. We might call them all portraits. They communicate the nature of the whole by attending to the uniqueness of each part, by choosing from among the parts certain of them for emphasis, and by modifying them and rearranging them in ways that satisfy the "feeling" of the portrayer.[1]

What does all this have to do with our desire to live full, fulfilling, and enjoyable lives? Actually, a great deal. Developing knowledge of the different cultures and civilizations of the world not only makes it possible for us to understand and appreciate these cultures and civilizations as wholes or total ways of life, but also for us to enrich our lives in countless ways. There is a wealth of information and insights to be gleaned from broadening and deepening our knowledge, understanding, and awareness of the world's cultures and civilizations in the holistic sense if we are wise enough to recognize this, especially with respect to different ways of seeing, acting, and valuing things in the world, accepting and appreciating others and their differences, expanding our consciousness and mindfulness, enhancing our welfare and well-being, and improving our individual and collective behavior and everyday actions.

This is also true with respect to our awareness and appreciation of nature. While the arts are not the only vehicle capable of doing this, it is remarkable how much can be learned about nature, the natural environment, and other species from the arts, as well as how imperative it is to revere nature and make it an integral part of our lives on a daily basis.

Consider what can be learned about the universe as a whole, the natural world, and other living species as an example. There is an incredible amount to be learned about these matters from Hildegard von Bingen's *Symphony of the Harmony of Heavenly Revelations*, Gustav Holst's *The Planets*, Franz Schubert's *Trout Quartet*, Charles-Camille Saint-Saëns' *Carnival of the Animals*, Alan Hovhanes' *Mysterious Mountain,* Claude Debussy's *La Mer* (*The Sea*), and countless others. This goal can also be achieved by studying the nature paintings of Claude Monet, Vincent van Gogh, and the host of other Impressionist artists, the poetry of William Wordsworth, Samuel Taylor Coleridge, Percy Bysshe Shelley, John Keats, and Walt Whitman, the writings of Ralph Waldo Emerson, Henry David Thoreau, and John Muir, the photographs of Ansel Adams, and the works of wildlife artists such as John James Audubon, Owen Gromme, Robert Bateman, and Glen Loates.

And this brings us, by a circuitous route, to the ability of the arts and artists to motivate, uplift, and inspire us, as well as to help us to reach above and beyond ourselves in the search for spirituality and the sublime. Together with holism, these two abilities may be the most important of all during the adult and final stages of our lives because they make it possible for us to achieve and experience things that at first sight seem impossible.

I have discovered over the course of my life that there are many works of art that motivate, uplift, and inspire me and I believe the same is true for all people. While particular works and specific art forms touch different people in different ways, I must confess that I am motivated, uplifted, and inspired whenever I hear the last movement of Saint-Saëns' *Organ Symphony* (*Symphony No. 3*), Sibelius's *Finlandia*, Handel's *Zadok the Priest*, Elgar's *Pomp and Circumstance March No. 1*, and Beethoven's *Appassionata* and *Waldstein* sonatas as well as the last movement of his *Moonlight Sonata,* which is completely different from the first movement. This is also true when I look at landscape paintings, such as Vincent van Gogh's *The Starry Night* and *Starry Night over the Rhône*, Claude Monet's *The Artist's Garden at Giverny* and *The Water Lily Pond*, as well as works by Canadian artists such as Tom Thomson's *Woodland Waterfall*, and *Autumn's Garland*, Arthur Lismer's *Bright Land*, A. Y. Jackson's *The Red Maple*, and Emily Carr's *The Forest, British Columbia*.

These experiences are multiplied many times over by artistic works that cause me to reach above and beyond myself in the search for the sublime. My experiences in this area are exhilarating and enthralling because they have propelled me to lofty heights on numerous occasions. Many of these works are in the field of music.

One night, I had a profound experience of this kind after I had gone to bed. I tuned my radio (as I do every night) to a station that plays soothing and serene music, and fell fast asleep. I don't know how long I was sleeping, but slowly I became aware that I was hearing one of the most exquisite pieces of music I have ever heard. I actually thought I had died and gone to heaven because the music was so beautiful, until I heard an announcer say, "You have been listening to *Grant Us Peace* by Felix Mendelssohn, sung by the Corydon singers." I have often thought this piece of music should be adopted as humanity's "universal anthem." Not only is it extremely beautiful, but it would also serve a very useful purpose. With all the violence, terrorism, conflict, systemic racism, and hostility in the world, its plea to "grant us peace" is not only very valuable but also extremely timely.

More recently, I had a similar experience with another piece of music on the radio, although this time it was early in the morning rather than late at night. While I set my alarm to let out a loud "beep" at precisely six o'clock every morning, for some curious reason I was awakened on this particular morning not by that "beep" but by another piece of music that was also sublime. When it was over, I listened attentively to find out what the piece was and who composed it. Unfortunately, I only caught about half of this. It sounded as though the announcer said, "You have just listened to a piece written by Robert Han [or was it Robert Hand?] for oboe and orchestra."

I immediately jumped out of bed, went to my computer, and began searching frantically for this piece. After a long and arduous search, I discovered it was "Ah Chloris," written by a composer I had never heard of named Reynaldo Hahn, who was born in Venezuela but spent most of his life in France. It is usually performed by either a solo singer or an oboe player with piano or small orchestral accompaniment. Do you know this exquisite piece of music? If you don't, you may want to listen to it as sung by Susan Graham.

The Lost Chord should also be added to this list. I discovered this piece quite by accident several years ago and it has been a favourite of mine ever since. It was composed by Sir Arthur Sullivan in 1877 during the illness and subsequent death of his brother. I was very surprised to learn Sullivan was the composer because, of course, he was one half of Gilbert and Sullivan, the team responsible for creating many comic operettas, including *The Pirates of Penzance*, *The Mikado*, and many others.

One of the most remarkable things about *The Lost Chord* is not only the captivating music but also the incredible words. They are from a poem written by Adelaide Anne Proctor. I quote them here in full because they are symbolic of the ability of some artists and arts organizations to open the door to the sublime and possibly even the divine, as well as to demonstrate the herculean heights to which the arts can soar in our lives:

> Seated one day at the organ, I was weary and ill at ease,
> And my fingers wander'd idly over the noisy keys;
> I knew not what I was playing, or what I was dreaming
> then,
> But I struck one chord of music like the sound of a great
> Amen.
>
> It flooded the crimson twilight like the close of an
> Angel's Psalm,
> And it lay on my fever'd spirit with a touch of infinite
> calm.
> It quieted pain and sorrow like love overcoming strife,
> It seem'd the harmonious echo from our discordant life.
>
> It link'd all perplexed meanings into one perfect peace,

And trembled away into silence as if it were loth to
cease;
I have sought, but I seek it vainly, that one lost chord
divine,
Which came from the soul of the organ and enter'd into
mine.

It may be that Death's bright Angel will speak in that
chord again;
It may be that only in Heav'n I shall hear that grand
Amen!

Having discussed the remarkable impact the arts can have in our childhood, youth, and adult lives, these inspirational words in *The Lost Chord* bring me to the two final stages of life. The first is usually referred to as "the retirement stage," although we must surely find a better term for it because that sounds as though life is more or less over by this point, which is anything but the case. In fact, this is an ideal time to be actively involved in the arts, especially if we haven't had the good fortune to be involved in them to any great extent earlier in life.

This involvement can be achieved on one's own or through such organizations as senior citizens' homes, seniors' groups, community centres, and others, all of which are rapidly increasing their arts offerings for people in this stage of life. As a result, these years are the perfect time to take up a musical instrument, paint pictures, sing in a choir, make craft objects, dance, enjoy humour and comedy, learn about the artistic and cultural heritages of different countries, acquaint oneself with outstanding works of art, and, in short, seek out all the pleasures the arts can bring us.

After this, there is life's "final stage." Contemporary research is revealing the arts have an essential role to play here as well, not only for people who are very elderly but otherwise healthy and able to enjoy life and the arts in many ways, but also—and especially—for people suffering from severe and debilitating diseases and illnesses such as cancer, heart disease, strokes, anxiety, depression, dementia, Alzheimer's, Parkinson's, multiple sclerosis, ALS, and so forth.

In recent years, there has been a phenomenal increase in the number of organizations, books, research studies, and other developments devoted to coming to grips with illnesses and diseases such as these and how they affect individuals at this stage in life. What has been discovered is that the arts can be very helpful in assisting people with devastating illnesses and diseases during the final stage of life. They can help people to hear better, remember more, express their creativity, improve their balance, and interact with others, by listening to music, singing songs, dancing alone or with others, recalling favourite tunes, melodies, and artistic experiences from the past, and a great deal else.

Countless hospitals, palliative care centres, and organizations like the Society for the Arts in Dementia Care, Partnerships in Dementia Care Alliance, the National Ballet School of Canada, and many others are doing research in this area. This research is discussed in such books as *The Creative Arts in Dementia Care: Practical Person-Centred Approaches and Ideas* by Jill Hayes and *Dementia Arts: Celebrating Creativity in Elder Care* by Gary Glazer. While the arts are not the only activities with the capacity to help the very elderly, and while they cannot cure these illnesses and diseases, they can make it easier for people to deal with them, as well as help caregivers and family members struggling to help people cope with some of life's greatest trials, tribulations, and ordeals.

When all the benefits to be derived from the arts at each and every age and stage in life are tallied up and considered collectively, it is clear that the arts must be viewed in a totally new light. After decades during which the importance of the arts was downplayed, it is now evident that they deserve a prominent place throughout one's life. Not only is this the solution to achieving more balance and harmony in one's life, but it is also the key to living a full, fulfilling, happy, and healthy life. There is simply no alternative or substitute.

Chapter 3
The Power of Music

I believe music has a powerful role to play in the development of our personalities and lives.

While this is a personal belief, I have encountered many people throughout the world who share it. Furthermore, there is mounting evidence to confirm it. There is something about music that broadens, deepens, and enriches our personalities and lives in countless ways, making it of crucial importance to people in all parts of the world regardless of what type of music they listen to or prefer.

This belief can be traced back to ancient times. The Greek philosopher Plato was a strong believer in the important role music can play in our lives, especially at an early age. Not only did he say, "I would teach children music, physics, and philosophy, but most importantly music, for the patterns in music and all the arts are the keys to learning," but also he believed that "musical training is a more potent instrument than any other, because rhythm and harmony find their way into the inward places of the soul, on which they mightily fasten." In *The Republic* Plato also said, "Music is a moral law. It gives soul to the universe, wings to the mind, flight to the imagination, and charm and gaiety to life and to everything." In fact, *The Republic* is filled with references to the powerful role music can play in the development of people, their personalities, and their lives, as well as the development of societies, nations, and the ideal state.

Recognition of the potential of music is not limited to Plato or to ancient times. Over the course of history, many individuals and institutions have recognized music's importance. In the nineteenth century, for instance, the American poet Henry Wadsworth Longfellow called music "the universal language of mankind" and the Danish author Hans Christian Andersen declared that "where words fail, music speaks." In both cases, it was felt that music possesses certain qualities and capabilities that make it in many ways even more important than language itself.

Contemporary research is revealing why it is that music plays such a strong role. Using functional magnetic resonance imaging (FMRI), scientists have discovered that music provides "a total workout for the brain" whereas most other activities provide only a "partial workout." Music performs this role by stimulating not just the brain and blood flow, but also the mind, body, senses, and all other human faculties. It also reduces anxiety, high blood pressure, and pain, improves sleep, and enhances mood, motivation, mental alertness, and memory. As such, it is an ideal activity for seniors and people suffering from many different illnesses and diseases as well as for children, teenagers, and adults.

Findings like these have been confirmed by the International Arts+Mind Lab at the Brain Science Institute at Johns Hopkins University's School of Medicine, as well as by Isabelle Peretz at the University of Montreal and Robert Zatorre at McGill University, who together created the International Laboratory for Brain, Music, and Sound Research to "study music as a portal into the most complex aspects of human brain functions."

And this is not all. Jonathan Burdette, a neuroradiologist at Wake Forest Baptist Medical Center, has conducted numerous studies of the effects of music on the brain. He has concluded that "it doesn't matter if it's Bach, the Beatles, Brad Paisley, or

Bruno Mars. Your favorite music likely triggers a similar type of activity in your brain as other people's favorites do in theirs. Music is primal. It affects all of us, but in very personal, unique ways. Your interaction with music is different than mine, but it's still powerful."

We have all been so touched by music that we feel we have transcended the world and entered a very special place. This is because music brings an enormous amount of joy and happiness into our lives and moves us in profound and captivating ways that reach right into our hearts, souls, and being. Musicians are fully aware of this, which is why they create sounds, rhythms, melodies, and compositions that produce musical experiences that resonate strongly with our feelings, emotions, hopes, dreams, fears, and aspirations, often in far-reaching, engaging, and mystical ways.

Just as Elizabeth Browning asked, "How do I love thee, let me count the ways?" so a similar question might be asked about music. And the answer is the same: music affects our personalities and lives in countless ways. There is music that satisfies our every mood, moment, and situation. It invigorates, stimulates, and motivates us, activates, agitates, and challenges us, soothes and relaxes us, excites and inspires us, enables us to soar to great heights, is incredibly beautiful, gives us a sense of awe, wonder, and ecstasy, is nostalgic, helps us to express our feelings, emotions, love, and compassion, connects us with other people, makes it possible to share experiences, depicts specific places and events, acts as a gateway to cultures, enhances our awareness and appreciation of nature, and a great deal else. I demonstrate these effects of music in this chapter by providing examples in each of these areas from my own personal experiences in the western musical tradition. However, I believe this is true for all peoples and their musical experiences and traditions.

Consider music that stimulates and invigorates us. There is an incredible amount of music that does so. This happens for me whenever I hear trumpet voluntaries such as those composed by Henry Purcell, Marc-Antoine Charpentier, Jeremiah Clarke, Johann Friedrich Fasch, and John Stanley. It also happens when I listen to Charles-Marie Widor's *Toccata* from his *Symphony No. 5,* J. S. Bach's *Toccata and Fugue in D Minor* played on the organ, and many other works.

There is also music that activates, agitates, and challenges us. This music is often concerned with social issues and political concerns. Some of the best-known examples of this are the activist activities and musical works of American folk singers such as Woodie Guthrie, Pete Seeger, the Weavers, Joan Baez, Bob Dylan, Peter, Paul, and Mary, Johnny Cash, and Bruce Springsteen. Each of these musicians, and many others, were involved in social and political causes during important stages in their lives that were designed to bring about change, especially during the Dirty Thirties, the Great Depression, the Vietnam War, the civil rights movement, and so forth. In the process, they created many popular songs, such as "Where Have All the Flowers Gone," "This Land Is Your Land," "Blowin' in The Wind," "If I Had a Hammer," "We Shall Overcome," "Born in the USA," and others.

What makes the activist activities of musicians so important is the fact that they challenge existing ways of doing things, create new practices, patterns, and possibilities, foster new relationships and associations, bring about transformation and change, and are provocative, as Stravinsky's *The Rite of Spring* was when first performed in Paris in 1913 and for some time thereafter. Such initiatives are needed more than ever in view of all the social, racial, and human inequalities and injustices that exist throughout the world today.

While many pieces of music stimulate, motivate, activate, and challenge us, others have a very different effect. They soothe and relax us, especially when we are uptight, distraught, or experiencing anxiety and apprehension. Whenever this happens to me, I usually listen to Rachmaninoff's *Second Piano Concerto*—as apparently many people do—and especially those remarkable chords at the very beginning of the first movement that set the stage for the entire composition. I am also soothed whenever I hear the second movements of Beethoven's *Fifth Piano Concerto* (mentioned earlier) as well as the second movement of his *Violin Concerto,* Cécile Chaminade's *Concertino for Flute and Orchestra,* Wagner's *Prelude* to *Lohengrin* and *Overture* to *Parsifal*, and Engelbert Humperdinck's "Evening Prayer" and "Dream Pantomine" from his *Hänsel and Gretel* opera. These pieces always calm me.

But there is also music that excites and inspires us. Choices here tend to be highly personal in nature, since what may excite and inspire one person may not excite and inspire another. Nevertheless, music of this type is extremely important because it often causes us to reach above and beyond ourselves in the search for the sublime. Personally, I am inspired whenever I hear Wagner's *Overture* to *Tannhäuser* and Ravel's orchestral version of Mussorgsky's *Pictures at an Exhibition*, to cite only two examples of many. This appears to be true for many other people. Here are a few comments posted on YouTube about Mussorgsky's monumental work: "This was my introduction to classical music seventy years ago. It helped change the life of a Chicago slum kid to one of culture and success." "Finishing my homework to the Great Gate of Kiev, I feel as if I have accomplished something important." "He based music on paintings. Very clever and very inspirational."

Music like this enables us to "soar to great heights" and "fly with the eagles." And this is not confined to classical music. A great deal of popular music does this for me and does it very well, most notably "You Raise Me Up" and "Wind Beneath My Wings" when they are sung by Josh Groban and Bette Midler respectively, as well as Elton John's captivating "Circle of Life."

To these examples must be added music that is very beautiful. Beauty is one of music's most powerful assets and cherished qualities. For music as in many other areas of life, beauty is in the eye—or should I say the ear, mind, heart, and soul—of the beholder. While some pieces of music are beautiful from beginning to end, others are beautiful only in specific parts. This is because it is very difficult to sustain beauty in music for a long period of time. Pieces that do so are usually quite short, such as Chopin's *Etude in A flat, Op. 25, No. 1* (Aeolian Harp), Bach's *Prelude No. 1*, Mozart's *Ave Verum Corpus*, Handel's *Minuet from Berenice,* Fauré's *Cantique de Jean Racine*, Liszt's transcription of Schumann's *Widmung*, Schubert's *Impromptu, No. 3 in G flat major*, and Richard Strauss' *Morgen.*

Music that is very beautiful often gives rise to a feeling of awe, wonder, and ecstasy, thereby occupying a special place in the development of our personalities and lives. Sacred and choral music does this for many people and does it very well; examples include the sacred and choral music of the Renaissance as well as composers such as Hildegard of Bingen, Corelli, Gabrieli, Palestrina, Monteverdi, Striggio, and Tallis and his ethereal *Spem in Alium.* Added to these would undoubtedly be Barber's *Agnus Dei*, Dvořák's "Song to the Moon," Franck's *Panis*

Angelicus, Bach's *Air on a G String*, and Morricone's *Gabriel's Oboe* and *Dinner* from his *La Califfa Suite*.

Then there is music that is nostalgic. This is one of the most fascinating but also frustrating things about music. This is because nostalgia—which comes in many different forms and is encountered in many diverse ways—is almost always bittersweet. Not only does it produce fond memories that flood into the mind, but it is tinged with a certain amount of sadness and sorrow because the events that gave rise to those memories can never be repeated again, regardless of how close they are or may seem. This is surely one of the most difficult things to come to grips with, since it feels as though we can actually reach out and relive these cherished moments from the past until reason and logic step in and remind us that they are gone forever. Nevertheless, we cherish them and constantly replay them in our minds and memories, as well as at concerts, because they are so precious.

There are countless songs that are nostalgic, such as "Time to Say Goodbye," "Londonderry Air" ("Danny Boy"), "Loch Lomond," "Auld Lang Syne," "Carrickfergus," "The Last Rose of Summer," "Shenandoah," "Return to Sorrento," "Goin' Home," "Ladies in Lavender," "She's Called Nova Scotia," "Ashokan Farewell," and many others. It is not coincidental that many of these songs are Scottish or Irish because Scotland and Ireland are filled with music of this type. This is probably because it was so difficult for people to eke out a living in these countries due to the inclement weather, tough terrain, geographical location, and isolation from the rest of Europe. Pieces like these always leave us hanging in some sense, since they are usually concerned with a family member, friend, loved one, group, or experience that may last forever in our minds but will never be experienced again in reality.

One of the reasons for nostalgia in music is that it is filled with a great deal of emotion. This is equally true for music that helps us to express our love, feelings, emotions, gratitude, affection, and appreciation. We have all had many experiences with music of this type.

This ability to express these qualities and sensations is evident in many pieces of music and every person has her or his favourites. A favourite of mine is "I'll Walk Beside You," written by Alan Murray and Edward F. Lockton many years ago and sung with great tenderness and affection by Bryn Terfel. This song was very popular during and after the Second World War when it was popularized by the great Irish tenor John McCormick.

This discussion of nostalgia is a perfect introduction to music that connects us to other people and enables us to share experiences. I am thinking here of such well-known pieces as Charlie Chaplin's "Smile," with memorable words by John Turner and Geoffrey Parsons; "Can You Feel the Love Tonight?" with music by Elton John and lyrics by Tim Rice; Louis Armstrong's rendition of "What a Wonderful World"; Handel's "Where'er You Walk"; and Jussi Björling and Robert Merrill's famous duet *Au Fond du Temple Saint* from Bizet's opera *Les Pêcheurs de Perles* (*The Pearlfishers*), as well as many others.

So far, we have been considering music that shapes and affects our personalities and lives in an internal sense. But there are also many types and pieces of music that do so in an external fashion. Whereas the first type of music is concerned with "the self," the second type is concerned with "the other," enabling us to get out of our own skins and into the world at large. Music that does this is often very revealing, since many composers have a knack for depicting people, events, experiences, stories, places, cultures, nature, and nature's diverse elements in highly descriptive, revealing, and compelling ways.

Take depictions of people as an example. Included here in real and imagined terms would undoubtedly be Aaron Copland's *Billy the Kid* and *Lincoln Portrait*, Richard Strauss' *Don Juan*, *Macbeth*, and *Till Eulenspiegel's Merry Pranks*, Tchaikovsky's *Romeo and Juliet Fantasy*, Rodrigo's *Fantasia para un gentilhombre*, and many others.

Telemann's *Don Quixote Suite* does this as well. This work is intriguing, not only because the music is so alluring, but also because Telemann depicts the hidalgo Alonso Quixano, his squire and peasant servant Sancho Panza, his worn-out horse Rosinante, and the love of his life Princess Dulcinea del Toboso, in a very masterful way. You can almost see Quixano on his steed in full armour, carrying his trusted sword and lance and tilting at windmills, attempting to revive chivalry in the world, undertaking heroic deeds to impress his lady love, and trying to overcome the many injustices in the world as the music unfolds and the depictions enable us to conjure up scenes and images of this type. The same descriptive ability is evident in some of Telemann's other music, most notably his *Tafelmusik* (*Music for the Table*), and *La Bourse* (*Stock Exchange*) *Suite*. It is easy when listening to these pieces to see people sitting around a dinner table enjoying good food and drink, as well as scurrying across the stock exchange floor buying and selling stocks and bonds. This same descriptive quality is evident in Wagner's *Overture to the Flying Dutchman*. It is easy to feel tossed around at sea in the middle of a treacherous storm while listening to this piece, and even to feel seasick to a certain extent. And what about Tchaikovsky's *1812 Overture*? Is there any better way to tell a story and describe an event without using any words and by employing music as the vehicle than this evocative work?

Paul Dukas' *The Sorcerer's Apprentice* should definitely be added to this list, especially as the apprentice tries frantically to mop up the water on the floor as the brooms multiply endlessly. The music served as the inspiration for one of the segments in Walt Disney's animated film *Fantasia*, created in 1940, with Mickey Mouse as the sorcerer's apprentice. Then there is Nikolai Rimsky-Korsakov's enticing composition *Scheherazade*. It is based on a story from *The Arabian Nights* about the daughter of a vizier who tells Sultan Shahryer a different story every night for a thousand and one nights to stave off execution, since she stops telling each story in the middle of the night. The Sultan is so anxious to hear the end of every story that he saves Scheherazade's life night after night. By the time she has exhausted all her stories, the Sultan is so deeply in love with her that he makes her his bride rather than executing her.

What is true for people, events, stories, and experiences is also true for places. A long list could be drawn up here as well, such as George Gershwin's *An American in Paris*, Ferde Grofé's *Grand Canyon Suite*, Rodrigo's *Concierto Aranjuez* and *Concierto Andaluz*, and such songs as "New York, New York," "Scarborough Fair," "I Love Paris," and many others. One composer who had a real penchant for depicting places in music is Albert Ketèlbey. Many of his compositions, such as *In a Monastery Garden*, *In a Persian Market*, *In a Chinese Temple Garden*, *In the Mystic Land of Egypt*, and *Bells Across the Meadow* are excellent illustrations of his ability to do this.

There are also many pieces of music that are symbolic of cultures or act as gateways to cultures, as noted earlier. I am thinking here of Joseph Canteloube's *Songs of the Auvergne*, which are representative of the culture of the Auvergne region in France, Borodin's *Polovtsian Dances* from *Prince Igor,* which are symbolic of the cultures of the Kipchaks and Cumans, a nomadic Turkish people, Max Bruch's *Scottish Fantasy,* Fritz Kreisler's *Tambourin Chinois,* and George Enescu's two *Romanian Rhapsodies, Op. 11.* While these pieces do not depict whole cultures, they do depict some of the most salient parts and revealing characteristics of cultures, making it possible to begin to piece together an image of what these cultures might be like in the holistic or all-encompassing sense.

Nowhere is the capacity that music possesses for depicting the world more apparent than with respect to nature and nature's diverse elements. Not only is music of this type capable of broadening and deepening our knowledge, understanding, and awareness of nature, but there is an incredible amount to be learned from music of this type about the natural world and how important it is to preserve, protect, and revere it. It is amazing how many composers have been concerned with nature over the centuries, creating a vast cornucopia of works concerned with the natural world in all its grandeur, complexity, and diversity.

Think, for example, of the *Sunrise Prelude* in Richard Strauss's *Also Sprach Zarathustra,* Henry Mancini and Johnny Mercer's *Moon River,* Beethoven's *Pastoral Symphony (Symphony No. 6),* Arnold Schoenberg's *Verklärte Nacht (Transfigured Night),* Benjamin Britten's *Four Sea Interludes,* Debussy's *Prélude á l'après-midi d'un faune (Prelude to the Afternoon of a Faun),* Edward Grieg's *Morning Mood* from his *Peer Gynt Suite,* Tchaikovsky's *Swan Lake,* Wagner's *Forest Murmurs,* Vincent d'Indy's *Symphony on a French Mountain Air,* Léo Delibes *Flower Duet* from *Lakmé,* Johann Strauss II's *Roses from the South Waltz,* and countless others.

The seasons figure prominently in music of this type. Many

composers, such as Haydn and Glazunov, have written music about the seasons, especially after Vivaldi set the stage with his remarkable *The Four Seasons.* This piece conveys the sense of excitement and anticipation that exists at the beginning of spring, the torrid heat and scorching sun of the summer, the beauty and melancholy of the fall with its exquisite colours, pungent aromas, and falling leaves, and the harshness of winter with its ice, snow, and bone-chilling cold.

Water and rivers are also a favourite subject of composers, perhaps because water is one of the world's most precious assets and there would be no life on the planet without it, and because rivers involve flow and movement, key aspects of personality development and the life process (and of music as well). Some of the best-known examples of musical treatments of this subject are Smetana's *The Moldau,* Johann Strauss II's *The Blue Danube,* and *Flow Gently, Sweet Afton* by Robert Burns and Jonathan Spilman, with its exquisite melody and the captivating words of the first verse:

> Flow gently, sweet Afton! amang thy green braes,
> Flow gently, I'll sing thee a song in thy praise;
> My Mary's asleep by thy murmuring stream,
> Flow gently, sweet Afton, disturb not her dream.

To these examples should be added Bruce Springsteen's popular song *The River,* as well as *The Rivers of Babylon* by Brent Dowe and Trevor McNaughton of the Jamaican Reggae group The Melodians. There are many other musical works written about various rivers, such as the Yellow River (or Huang He) in China, the Seine and Loire rivers in France, the Rhine River in Germany, the Nile in Egypt, the Ganges in India, the mighty

Mississippi in the United States, and long-time favourites such as *Ol' Man River* and *Shenandoah.* And what about Handel's *Water Music*? While it was not written with a specific river in mind, it was written to be performed on a barge floating down a very famous river—the Thames River in England—and had to be repeated many times because King George I enjoyed it so much.

Animals also form a very important element in the works of many composers. A long list could be drawn up here as well, such as Saint-Saëns' *Carnival of the Animals,* Ralph Vaughan Williams' *The Lark Ascending*, Stravinsky's *Firebird*, Bach's *Sheep May Safely Graze*, Prokoviev's *Peter and the Wolf*, Ravel's *Mother Goose Suite*, Rimsky-Korsakov's *The Flight of the Bumble Bee*, and many others. Numerous composers have also had a special fascination with birds, which, when they sing and chirp, also create music. As a result, many composers have used birds and bird calls in their music, most notably Janequin in *Le Chant des Oiseaux* (*Bird Calls*), Handel in *The Cuckoo and the Nightingale*, Respighi in *Gli uccelli* (*The Birds*), Olivier Messiaen in *Oiseaux Exotiques* (*Exotic Birds*), Germaine Tailleferre in *Le Marchand d'oiseaux* (*Trader of Birds*), as well as Vivaldi in his remarkable *Concerto in D, Op. 10/3,* nicknamed "the Goldfinch," with its remarkable bird imitations, and music by Mozart inspired by his pet starling.

I could go on, but the point has been made. Not only is there a great deal of music to suit our every mood, occasion, and situation, but there is also an incredible amount of music that enables us to go deeper into the self as well as learn more about other people and the world at large. Indeed, there is very little in the world that is not connected to music or cannot be explained or understood through music in one form or another.

Even if we went no further than this, it is apparent that music plays a powerful role in our personality development and lives. In the process of perpetually expanding our involvement in music—all types of music and not just classical, popular, or folk music—it is possible to reap enormous benefits and rewards, as lovers of music (and hopefully participants in music) are discovering, regardless of whether this means listening to music, playing a musical instrument, singing in a choir, or engaging in some other form of musical activity and music-making.

But this is by no means the end of the story. Music can also act as a springboard for transforming our personalities and lives in many other ways, enabling us to strive for a much higher level of existence and deeper form of consciousness. Not only can music commence the process that is needed to make us "whole people"—people who have achieved oneness and unity among all our different faculties—but it can also help us to live in harmony with other people, other cultures, other religions, and other species, as well as the natural environment. In doing so, it can make us full and centred people, as well as altruistic, compassionate, sensitive, and humane. This enables us to experience more meaning, purpose, and spirituality in life, as well as develop all the qualities and capabilities required for a healthy and fulfilling life.

Just as providing specific examples is helpful in understanding how music can broaden, deepen, and enrich our personalities and lives, providing similar illustrations of people who have used music to achieve outstanding things can be equally helpful. While I can think of many people who fit this description, the one who stands out most in my mind in this respect is Albert Schweitzer.

Schweitzer was a student of music, a musician, and an organist long before he became a theologian, philosopher, humanitarian, and physician. Born in France in 1875, he studied music and took organ lessons in Mulhouse from 1885 to 1893, and also learned to play the piano. He was especially knowledgeable about the life and musical works of Johann Sebastian Bach and even wrote a two-volume book about Bach and his musical accomplishments. During this time but especially later in life, he studied theology, philosophy, and medicine, and obtained degrees in theology and medicine from the University of Strasbourg.

In 1913, Schweitzer left his musical career and Europe behind him and went to Africa to create and develop the Albert Schweitzer Hospital in Lambaréné, now in Gabon in west-central Africa. He spent many decades there treating thousands of patients suffering from different illnesses and diseases. When this was no longer possible because of his age and some health problems, he divided his time between Africa and Europe for the remainder of his life. Interestingly, he had a piano created for him that was designed especially for the tropics; he played every day after lunch as well as on Sundays.

Schweitzer received the Nobel Peace Prize in 1952 for his personal and professional accomplishments and commitment to "reverence for life" and "the necessity of ethics and ethical behavior in society." While he has been criticized for his paternalistic attitude towards Africans and the lack of proper sanitation in his hospital, he laboured for more than fifty years in Africa as a medical doctor and humanitarian, treating sick people under extremely difficult conditions. When he was no longer able to do this, he fought against nuclear weapons, feeling they were contrary to his belief that all life is precious and that everything that advances life is good and everything that degrades it is bad.

By expanding and enriching life in virtually all directions and in every possible way, Schweitzer provides an excellent example of how our personalities and lives can be enriched and transformed by using music as a springboard. Schweitzer described what life and living can and should be all about when viewed from a cultural perspective:

> The ripeness that our development must aim at is one which makes us simpler, more truthful, purer, more peace loving, meeker, kinder, more sympathetic.... That is the process in which the soft iron of youthful idealism hardens into the steel of a full-grown idealism which can never be lost.[2]

Schweitzer was not the only person to use music as a springboard for transforming his personality and life and achieving many important things. Nor is music the only art form capable of doing this. However, doing so allows us to reap the full advantages and immense benefits that can be derived from music and all the other arts, making it possible to live one's life on a much higher plane—something that may be needed more than ever in the world of the future.

Chapter 4
The Future of Arts Education

To begin with, let's start with the context of arts education. This is because context plays a crucial role in determining the contents of arts education, as it does in virtually all other disciplines and areas of life.

There is no doubt about what the most important factor was in determining the present context of arts education. It was the publication of C. P. Snow's book *The Two Cultures and the Scientific Revolution* in 1959.[3]

In this book, Snow made the case that intellectual life in the western world was divided into two cultures—the artistic-humanistic culture and the scientific culture. This was a real hindrance in coming to grips with the world's problems at that time, according to Snow, because he believed that the artistic-humanistic culture was given far too much attention and the scientific culture far too little attention in western countries and their educational systems.

Snow made such a powerful case for giving more attention to the sciences and a scientific education in the western world that a shift began to occur away from the arts, humanities, and an artistic-humanistic education and towards the sciences and a scientific education. It wasn't long after this that the sciences came to be treated as "hard" subjects and the arts and humanities as "soft" subjects. This was accompanied by an increase in funding for the sciences and scientific education and a decrease in funding for the arts, humanities, and artistic-humanistic education in most educational institutions in the western world.

If this practice had been limited to educational institutions in the western world, Snow's position might not have had the powerful impact it eventually had in determining the present context of arts education. But it was not to be. Not long after this practice commenced, it became popular in the western world *as a whole*. This was because science was linked to economics, politics, industry, and technology, and therefore the conviction of businessmen, politicians, civil servants, corporations, and governments that this was the key to solving the world's problems, much as Snow had contended. It was also seen by such people as a way of reinforcing the economic age that had commenced with the publication of Adam Smith's *The Wealth of Nations* in 1776 but had stalled in the middle of the twentieth century with the stock market crash of 1929, the Great Depression from 1929 to 1939, the Second World War from 1939 to 1945, and the problems of post-war recovery in much of the world after that. It was time to get things back on track.

By this time, it was no longer a case of treating the sciences as hard subjects and the arts and humanities as soft subjects. More fundamentally, it was a case of treating the sciences as "hard activities" and the arts and humanities as "soft activities." Such views not only became firmly entrenched in the minds of businessmen, politicians, civil servants, and politicians, but also in the minds of countless citizens. With this, the "Snow thesis"—as it was called at that time and is still called today—became a societal phenomenon and not just an educational phenomenon. Hard activities were concerned with "the basics in life" and what life and living were really all about; soft activities were concerned with "the frills in life" and what people did in their "spare time." Seen this way, artistic and humanistic activities were appropriate as leisure activities, but had little to do with the necessities of life. Their purpose was to "round people out" and make them more civilized and sophisticated, as well as provide them with the knowledge and skills needed to prevent them from becoming bored in life and capable of better enjoying their free time.

When Snow saw what was happening after *The Two Cultures and the Scientific Revolution* was published in 1959, he wrote a second book on this subject in 1963 called *The Two Cultures: And a Second Look: An Expanded Version of the Two Cultures and the Scientific Revolution*.[4] In this book, Snow attempted to explain his case for the sciences and a scientific education in much more detail, as well as rectify the rift that had developed between the arts and humanities on the one hand and the sciences on the other hand. However, it was too late. The pendulum was swinging away from the arts and humanities and towards the sciences and Snow was powerless to prevent it, as often happens in situations that become polarized like this.

In the years that followed, courses and programs in the arts began to be cut in many educational jurisdictions throughout the world because a much lower priority was placed on them compared to the sciences. This worsened in the final decades of the twentieth century and first decades of the twenty-first, especially as this practice became entrenched in corporations, governments, ministries of education, and educational institutions in all parts of the world.

As this occurred, arts educators found themselves in a very difficult position as they were forced to decide what courses and programs should be cut and which ones should be maintained. With the arts treated largely as entertainment and leisure-time activities—and valued primarily for their economic impact in the economic age people were living in at that time and are still living in today—arts educators had to make the best of a terrible situation. This was not an easy task, since the context of arts education was stacked against them. Nevertheless, they fought back, and began to justify arts education courses and programs not only for their ability to teach students to play musical instruments, paint pictures, act in plays, dance, sing in choirs, write, and also as preparation for enjoying the arts later in life, but also for their capacity to address important social and cultural issues and stimulate creativity.

An excellent example of this "added dimension of arts education" was the creation of the "Seoul Agenda" by delegates at the Second World Conference on Arts Education convened by UNESCO in Seoul, South Korea in 2010. Included among the goals and objectives of the Seoul Agenda were:

- To apply arts education principles and practices to contribute to resolving the social and cultural challenges facing today's world;
- To support and enhance the role of arts education in the promotion of social responsibility, social cohesion, cultural diversity, and intercultural dialogue; and
- To affirm arts education as the foundation for balanced creative, cognitive, emotional, aesthetic, and social development of children, youth, and lifelong learning.

This describes the present context of arts education in most parts of the world today. It is a context that is heavily oriented towards seeing and treating arts education as a soft activity and arts courses and programs as soft courses and programs, preparing students for living in an economic age where the arts are valued primarily for their leisure-time applications, economic benefits, ability to entertain people, and more recently, their capacity to come to grips with socio-cultural issues and stimulate individual and collective creativity.

This context manifests itself most conspicuously today in what in most educational institutions and systems throughout the world is called STEM—Science, Technology, Engineering, and Mathematics.[5] In Canada, where I live, students in secondary school talk about the need to take the "six pack"—three science and three math credits—if they want to get into a good university, receive more job offers, land a better job, bring home a bigger pay cheque, and enjoy a higher standard of living and quality of life. This is endorsed by many parents, who are reluctant to see their children get involved in arts education and pursue a career in the arts.

This attitude says a great deal about "the image of the educated person" that is promoted and entrenched in today's economic age. It is an image based on the concept of "economic man" or "economic personality." This is a person or personality concerned primarily with the production and consumption of goods and services and creation of material and monetary wealth—as well as the maximizing of consumer satisfaction in the marketplace—in order to keep economies functioning effectively and growing at a rapid rate.

The problem with this image is that it is not compatible with the type of individual or educated person who is needed if we are to be successful in coming to grips with the life-threatening problems and challenges that exist throughout the world today. Clearly a new image of that person or personality in general—and the education of this person or personality in particular—is needed to come to grips with these problems and challenges.[6]

Fortunately for arts education and arts educators, "the moving finger writes, and having writ, moves on," as the Persian poet Omar Khayyam said in his poem "The Rubáiyát," translated into English by Edward FitzGerald in 1859. Clearly the moving finger is writing—and writing a great deal these days—as well as moving on and exposing some exceedingly difficult and dangerous problems in the process.

Over the last few decades, powerful signals have been emitted everywhere in the world that the economic age is not capable of coming to grips with these problems. Not only is it having a devastating effect on the natural environment and producing colossal inequalities in income and wealth, but it is not capable of coming to grips with such matters as the COVID-19 pandemic, health care crises, and the hostilities and conflicts that have arisen in many parts of the world due to the interaction and intermingling of people, groups, races, cultures, and religions with very different worldviews, values, customs, traditions, beliefs, and ways of life. The economic age is designed to produce goods, services, and material and monetary wealth, not to come to grips with problems as vast, vital, life-threatening, complex, and multidimensional as these.

To do so, it is necessary to pass out of the economic age and into a cultural age. Not only would a cultural age provide a much more effective context for dealing with these and other problems—especially when culture is defined and dealt with in holistic terms as a complex whole or total way of life—but it would also provide a much better context for developing the arts in general and arts education in particular. This is because the principal priority in a cultural age would be to achieve balance and harmony between all the many different factors, forces, disciplines, and activities that constitute global development and human affairs. In addition to this, there has been an intimate connection and inexorable bond between the arts and culture dating back to classical times.[7]

Just as the economic age has an image of the educated person buried deep within it, so does a cultural age. This latter image is concerned with the education of "the whole person" or "the cultural personality," and therefore with people who are holistic, centred, creative, altruistic, and humane.[8] This is necessary to achieve more happiness, fulfilment, and spirituality in life, as well as to live in harmony with the natural environment and other people, races, religions, countries, cultures, and species. It is also required to develop different worldviews, value systems, mindsets, and modes of behaviour than the ones that exist today, as well as the new skills and abilities needed if people are to function effectively in a cultural age and such an age is to provide an effective context for arts education and other disciplines as well.

There are many signs that confirm that things are moving in a favourable direction in this regard. One of the most important signs is the rapidly evolving realization that the arts in general —and arts education in particular—have an essential role to play at all stages and ages in the life process, from the earliest signs of life to its final days. And this is not all. There are also indications that the arts and arts education have a key role to play in coming to grips with many different types of illnesses and diseases, such as strokes, depression, anxiety, autism, Parkinson's, ALS, Alzheimer's, and many others, as discussed earlier.

What is ironic about this is the fact that the sciences are playing a very important role in this regard. This is because they are shedding a great deal of light on the nature and functioning of the human brain, the interaction that goes on between the right and left hemispheres of the brain, and the necessity of achieving balance and harmony between the two hemispheres of the brain in order to achieve good health and overall well-being.[9]

As documented earlier, scientists involved in functional magnetic resonance imaging (FMRI), as well as the scientific studies and empirical experiments being carried out at the International Arts+Mind Lab of the Brain Science Institute at the Johns Hopkins School of Medicine through its "research-to-practice initiatives" and what is called "neuroaesthetics," are revealing that this is not only true for music, but also for other art forms. Take the visual arts as another excellent illustration of this. Scientific research has confirmed that paintings enhance many brain functions by having an impact on brainwave patterns and emotions, the nervous system, and increased serotonin levels, as well as neural systems that yield a broad range of additional benefits such as improved motor skills, creativity, and emotional harmony. This is not all. Research undertaken by Professor Semir Keki, chair in neuroaesthetics at University College, London, has revealed that "whether it is a landscape, a still life, an abstract, or a portrait" that people are looking at, "there is a strong activity in that part of the brain that is related to pleasure." When people look at paintings, and especially beautiful paintings, blood flow increases in certain parts of the brain very considerably.[10]

These studies, and many others, confirm that the arts and sciences—like arts education and science education—are mutually complementary rather than mutually exclusive as well as cooperative rather than competitive when it comes to researching and finding solutions to a whole set of basic human problems and improving people's health and general well-being. In other words, the pendulum has started to swing back towards the centre rather than remaining stuck on one side, just as most people in the arts and very likely many people in the sciences had hoped. One organization that knew about this all along and incorporated it into their work is the Scientific Research Institute of Spiritual Development of Man and the associated UNESCO Chair in "Spiritual and Cultural Values of Upbringing and Education" at the Volodymyr Dahl East Ukrainian University in Kyiv, Ukraine. This organization has been providing courses and programs, undertaking research, disseminating information about their scientific and artistic findings, convening conferences, and producing informative publications in this area for several decades, thereby enhancing collective knowledge and understanding of the rich cornucopia of artistic and scientific benefits that can and are being derived from this approach.

Studies and findings like this, and many others that are now taking place throughout the world, confirm that the time is ripe to visualize and deal with arts education in a whole new way in educational systems and institutions around the globe.

Rather than cutting back on arts education courses and programs, it is time to broaden, deepen, diversify, and intensify arts education in elementary, secondary, post-secondary, and adult education institutions and learning centres throughout the world. Not only does a cultural age provide a much better context and fit for arts education in this sense, but it confirms that the arts have a central rather than marginal role to play as "drivers" of cultural activities and "exemplars" of cultural experiences.

Many developments are required in educational systems and

institutions around the world if this role is to be realized. One is broadening the scope of arts education, from the traditional performing, exhibiting, and literary arts to the cinematic, photographic, architectural, design, environmental, culinary, material, and language arts, as well as a deeper consideration of what different countries deem to be art forms in the first place. In Japan, for example, tree-dwarfing and flower-arranging are deemed to be art forms, just as calligraphy is in China and tattooing is in Tanzania. There is an enormous amount to be learned from each and every one of these art forms, and others like them such as the horticultural arts, that may appear less frequently on the list but are very important in the diverse and globalized world we are living in today.

What is true for the scope of arts education is also true for artistic styles. This is especially important with respect to what are usually referred to as the "classical" and "popular" arts. Surely the time has come to incorporate the more popular arts into arts education. These art forms include folk music, folk art, film music, art in public places, street theatre, wall murals, pop music, country music, ethnic dancing, and so forth. There is a great deal to be learned from these many different styles. This can be achieved by understanding the social barriers and class structures that have been created over the centuries that separate these different styles, as well as focusing attention on the many pedagogical benefits and educational rewards that accrue from this. To paraphrase Leonard Cohen (composer of "Hallelujah") in his popular song "Anthem," there are no perfect art forms but, rather, "a crack in everything"—and that's what lets in the light.

Added to this are all the different artistic genres. If, as the saying goes, "all is known by comparison," then it makes sense to compare and contrast different genres, especially genres popular during diverse periods of history and in various parts of the world. What are the similarities and differences, for example, between the arts in the ancient, medieval, early modern, and contemporary periods of history in different parts of the world, as well as between musical and visual art genres in different countries in the world during this time? What are the major differences between occidental and oriental art, or, to push this point a bit further, between music as it evolved in England, Germany, France, Spain, Russia, and Japan over the last four centuries? What do these differences say about other aspects of the cultures of these countries, as well as their different styles of living and ways of life?

Then there is the creative dimension of arts education. While most arts education programs around the world are strong in the performing, exhibiting, literary, and presentational side of the arts, they are often weak on the creative side, due largely to the fact that less attention has been paid to this particular dimension of the arts in both the historical and contemporary sense. This has been addressed in music education by the Canadian composer, author, and educator R. Murray Schafer, who has worked as a composer in many classrooms in elementary, secondary, and post-secondary schools in Canada, United States, Europe, and South America. As a composer, he took an approach to music education based much more on exploring sound, sounds, soundscapes, and composing music than on melodies, learning to play musical instruments, and performing music. While his approach was strongly criticized and resisted at the beginning, the international popularity of his many books on this subject—including *Composer in the Classroom, Ear Cleaning: Notes for an Experimental Music Course, Creative*

Music Education: A Handbook for the Modern Music Teacher, and especially *The Thinking Ear: Complete Writings on Music Education*—confirm that there is a great deal to be learned from taking a compositional approach to music education and not just a performing or presentational approach.

In a comprehensive, full-fledged arts education curriculum of the type advocated here, a great deal of consideration would also be given to the multiplicity of ways in which the arts enhance and enrich our knowledge, understanding, awareness, and appreciation of both the natural and human-made worlds.

As far as the natural world is concerned, the mind boggles at how many artistic works have been created that are concerned with this world in all its diverse forms and dimensions, and especially with how it manifests itself, creates communication among its myriad different elements and components, and connects everybody and everything in countless ways. There are millions of artistic works that do this, such as the constellation of works that are concerned with nature's diverse elements as well as trees, forests, rivers, plants, and animals that were discussed earlier. While these works provide an incredible amount of pleasure in a recreational and entertainment sense—is there anything more enjoyable than listening to Vivaldi's *The Four Seasons* in a concert hall or while sitting in one's living room or study at home?—they also expand our knowledge, understanding, and affection for the natural world immensely, especially at a time when we are losing contact with nature and the natural environment as a result of increased urbanization and developments in contemporary technology.

This brings us to the human-made world, which is also composed of countless elements, ingredients, and complex entities such as towns, cities, countries, cultures, civilizations, and the universal cultural heritage of humankind. There is a vast reservoir of artistic works here that can not only be enjoyed and appreciated, but also studied in great depth through the arts. The arts teach us a great deal about how past and present generations in every part of the world have imprinted and are imprinting their thoughts, ideas, creativity, culturescapes, and beliefs on specific areas of the world's geography.

This is especially true for artistic works that are symbolic of towns, cities, rural areas, countries, cultures, civilizations, and the cultural heritage of humankind in the holistic and all-encompassing sense. Just as a picture is worth a thousand words, so are works of art created by painters, playwrights, choreographers, composers, filmmakers, photographers, and so forth. They act as "gateways" to these collective cultural creations as dynamic and organic wholes and total ways of life that are constantly evolving, mutating, transforming, and transcending.

No person has contributed more to our knowledge and understanding of this miraculous symbolic process and holistic capability than the American documentary filmmaker Ken Burns. He has demonstrated an uncanny knack for selecting works in the arts—as well as specific events, people, and achievements—that are not only significant in their own right, but also representative of American culture in the all-encompassing sense. This is evident in all of his films, but especially in such films as *Country Music*, *Jazz*, *Baseball*, *The Civil War*, *The West*, *The Roosevelts*, *The Statue of Liberty*, and *The National Parks: America's Best Idea*. It is impossible to watch these films, and others like them, without learning an enormous amount about American culture as a whole and as a total way of life.

This is also true for the works of many other American artists, including Andy Warhol, Jackson Pollock, and Georgia O'Keeffe through their paintings, as well as Richard Rodgers, Oscar Hammerstein II, Irving Berlin, Aaron Copland, Leonard Bernstein, and a host of others through their music and especially such favourites as *The Sound of Music*, "God Bless America," "White Christmas," *Appalachian Spring*, *West Side Story*, and countless others. Not only do these works transport us into the heart and soul of American culture, but they convey a great deal about what this culture and way of life are really all about in the all-inclusive sense.

And what is true for American culture and the American way of life is also true for all other cultures and their ways of life, as well as the indispensable role the arts, artists, and arts organizations play in this symbolic and all-embracing process. This should be one of the principal goals of all arts educators and arts courses and programs in the future—to teach students to construct portraits of their own cultures and the cultures of other countries in the world as wholes through symbolic works of art by their own artists and other artists by means of this representative process.

Finally, there is the cultural heritage of humankind. Due to countless technological advances and the work of UNESCO and many other organizations over the last five or six decades, it is now possible for teachers and students in every country and school in the world—as well as at every level of the educational system and spectrum—to gain access to and retrieve information about virtually every element and item in this heritage. Not only is this a remarkable achievement today, but it promises to become even more remarkable in the future. This is where the tangible and intangible heritages of all the diverse countries of the world—

historic monuments and sites, cherished urban and rural areas, artistic districts and hubs, priceless architectural masterpieces, exquisite poems, paintings, stories, songs, plays, and dances, captivating and challenging games, literary heavyweights, oral traditions, and so forth—come to light and shine brightly in the world. Should this not also be an indispensable part of arts education in the years, decades, and centuries ahead?

While all people would benefit immensely from the type of comprehensive arts education advocated here, it would be particularly helpful to young people and future generations. Through teachers, courses, cellphones, iPads, computers, social platforms, and cultural networks, they will be able to gain access to virtually every historical and contemporary work of art by every artist of any age, type, or status in the world. My own experiences in arts education as well as studies in culture and cultures over many decades have convinced me that artistic, educational, and cultural experiences such as these are capable of producing exquisite sensations, powerful thoughts and images, creative ideas, spiritual states, and transcendental experiences that are without equal and border on the sublime and occasionally the divine. Such experiences carry with them no risks or dangers, as most drugs do, but give rise to countless rewards and benefits that can be enjoyed, cherished, and capitalized on over a lifetime.

One doesn't have to stretch the mind or imagination very far to visualize the multitude of opportunities and benefits that can be derived by people of all ages and classes in all parts of the world from arts courses, programs, and curricula of the type recommended here. Not only will such education enhance people's knowledge and understanding of their own culture and the cultures of others, thereby reducing the tensions and conflicts that often result from the inability to understand and accept the different cultures and civilizations of the world and their diverse worldviews, values, behaviors, attitudes, and motivations, but it will also open the doors to a vast array of possibilities to enjoy and experience.

We have progressed in broadening, deepening, diversifying, and intensifying arts education throughout the world long enough to realize how valuable and timely further steps will be in coming to grips with some of humanity's greatest problems and most fundamental needs going forward into the future. Not only will doing so open up a whole new era in the history of the arts and arts education, but it will also come at a time that is of vital importance to humanity and the history of the world.

Chapter 5
The Arts and Cities

When the city ceases to be a symbol of art and order, it acts in a negative fashion: it expresses and helps to make more universal the fact of disintegration.
—Lewis Mumford[11]

Suddenly cities are all the rage. After several decades of preoccupation with globalization and international trade, attention is shifting to cities as the new spawning grounds for innovative, dynamic, and creative activity.

In Canada, bank presidents are speaking out about the importance of cities, newspapers are calling for a new financial deal for cities, and governments are producing major reports and convening conferences on the development of cities. In United States, concerted attempts are being made to revitalize American cities after decades of decline and neglect. In Europe, competition is keen to create “cities of culture” and become “European cultural capitals.” And in Africa, Asia, South America, the Caribbean, and the Middle East, cities are growing rapidly in size and stature and the arts and culture are playing a very important role in this.

Why all the sudden interest in cities? There are many reasons. More than 55 percent of the world’s total population of 7.8 billion in 2020 is now living in cities and this number is expected to increase to 68 percent by 2050. Moreover, more and more people are looking to cities to solve their economic, environmental, medical, health, educational, social, and spiritual problems, as well as recognizing that it is the quality of life in cities that is the decisive factor. If cities lack the prerequisites for people to live a happy, healthy, sustained, and secure existence, no amount of national or international development will make up the difference.

Added to this is the dialectical reaction to globalization. This is manifesting itself in countervailing measures aimed at restoring people's sense of identity, belonging, solidarity, and control over the planning systems and decision-making processes affecting their lives. Finally, there is concern over the present state and future prospects for cities. Many feel cities lack the constitutional powers, fiscal arrangements, taxation capabilities, and institutional mechanisms that are required to deal with a whole host of complex urban problems, such as poverty, pollution, unemployment, homelessness, lack of low-cost housing, pressure on public facilities, over-burdened health care services and hospitals, transportation gridlock, soaring maintenance costs, environmental deterioration, and the need for more security, safety, and protection from dangerous diseases.

With this rapidly escalating interest in cities have come attempts to determine what it is that makes cities "livable." Why is living in one city debilitating and degrading whereas living in another city is exhilarating and exciting?

There are many reasons for this. One is stimulating employment opportunities and job prospects. Another is excellent educational institutions. Still others are superb medical facilities and health care services, effective transportation systems, numerous possibilities for accommodation, attractive parks, zoos, and recreational areas, a diversity of sports, recreational, and entertainment activities, superb restaurants, inspiring architectural features and historical sites, fascinating neighbourhoods, favourite haunts and hideaways, pride of place, and captivating ways to idle away the time of day. People take all these factors, and others, into account when deciding where to live, work, and settle down.

The arts make a major contribution to the development of cities that are livable in this sense. For one thing, they bring happiness to millions of people every year through concerts, plays, poetry readings, operas, art exhibits, films, festivals, and so forth. Many people will not locate in cities that lack high-quality artistic organizations and activities, especially art galleries, museums, theatre and dance companies, symphony orchestras, and arts and cultural centres.

The arts also contribute to the cohesion and social fabric of cities. They do so through their ability to engage large number of people in the artistic process, both as audience members and participants. In Sélestat, France at the turn of the century, for instance, the whole community came together and was actively involved in an exciting artistic undertaking called *Two Thousand Sounds for the Year 2000*. It was organized by skilled animators, the Maison de la Culture, and initiated by the mayor. It involved many artistic activities in different locations throughout the city and culminated with a huge artistic celebration in the central square.

Added to this is the valuable contribution the arts make to the economic development of cities. This happens through their ability to generate billions of dollars of investment and expenditure on facilities, equipment, hotels, restaurants, admissions, clothing, transportation, tourism, and the like. And this is not all. The arts also attract businesses, industries, and skilled labour forces. The most obvious examples of this in Canada are the Stratford Festival in Stratford, Ontario and the Shaw Festival in Niagara-on the-Lake, Ontario. The contributions the arts have made to the economies of these cities over a long period of time are well-documented and readily apparent, due largely to the fact that the arts have helped immensely to transform both these places into thriving centres. And what is true for Stratford and Niagara-on-the Lake is also true for many other cities across Canada as well as in many other countries, which is why corporations and industries often refuse to locate in cities that lack stimulating artistic experiences and numerous artistic resources.

The arts also contribute to the beautification and aesthetic features and ambiance of cities. They do this through many different activities, not just the activities of large professional arts organizations. Community arts councils and art centres, neighbourhood arts festivals, murals on the sides of buildings as well as on walls, buskers on city streets, the environmental, architectural, landscaping, and horticultural arts, as well as the material arts or crafts add richness, vitality, variety, and originality to urban settings and their surroundings. So do the works of children and young people. Is there anything more enjoyable than a children's art exhibition at the local community centre, a high school play, a choir performing at the town hall, or an annual music night?

The arts also contribute a great deal to harmony and cross-cultural communication, understanding, and exchange in cities. They bring people together in peaceful rather than violent ways and make it possible to communicate across ethnic, racial, and linguistic divides in profound, moving, memorable, and human ways. This will be increasingly important in a world where racial, ethnic, and religious tensions are mounting daily and at a rapid rate.

Then there is the contribution the arts make to the uniqueness, distinctive nature, and personalities of cities. As Amos Rapoport puts it, "Cities look, smell, sound and *feel* different; they have a different character or *ambience*."[12] Seen from this perspective, what would Paris be without the Eiffel Tower and the Louvre, New York without Broadway, off-Broadway theatre, and the New York Philharmonic, Beijing without the Forbidden City, and Bilbao without the Guggenheim Museum? Talk about uplifting city residents, tourists, and appreciating the uniqueness of cities!

While the arts make significant contributions to cities in all these different areas, their contributions do not end here. Recent research is revealing that the arts contribute to the development and livability of cities in other vitally important ways.

One of these ways is through the creative energy and synergy they inject into all aspects of urban life. By creating many of the concepts, contents, contexts, styles, methods, and techniques that are needed to institute change, artists and arts organizations pave the way for many other types of developments. It is not surprising in this regard that increasing numbers of civic planners and policy-makers are focusing their attention on the role that the "creative industries" play in urban development—creative industries such as the arts, education, the mass media, communications, and micro-enterprises that produce "clustering effects" and "convergent capabilities" that link different sectors and segments of cities together.[13] While there is a great deal of talk these days about "creative cities" and "creative economies," this is not possible without the arts. The arts make it possible for cities to be diverse, balanced, and integrated wholes rather than fragmented, disconnected, and unrelated parts.

Equally important is the contribution the arts make to the revitalization, renewal, and revival of cities. This has been realized in many cities in North America and Europe in recent years, largely through the creation of cultural hubs, districts, and capitals that have injected new life into cities after decades of disintegration, decay, and decline. These hubs, districts, and capitals involve constellations of artistic, athletic, heritage, media, entertainment, and commercial activities in strategic locations in cities, not only in downtown cores but also in other areas as well. Inspired by arts animators, administrators, entrepreneurs, corporate executives, educators, politicians, and citizens, these hubs, districts, and capitals have done a great deal to rejuvenate cities that have been dying from the inside out.

Canada provides an interesting and informative example of the artistic and cultural transformations that are occurring and required at the neighbourhood, community, and municipal level in virtually all parts of the world today. In Toronto, for instance, this transformation is being driven by a broad array of artists and arts organizations and is stimulating a great deal of innovative commercial, industrial, residential, tourist, and entrepreneurial activity. This includes recent developments and renovations to the Art Gallery of Ontario, the Royal Ontario Museum, and the Ontario College of Art and Design; the creation of the Distillery District and Liberty Village in former (and long neglected) industrial areas; creation of a major "cultural corridor" along Bloor Street that is linking together the Royal Ontario Museum, Bata Shoe Museum, Gardiner Museum, University of Toronto, Royal Conservatory of Music, Koerner Hall, and other institutions; as well as captivating developments in and around Ryerson University that include a remarkable make-over of Maple Leaf Gardens and a host of other innovative accomplishments in the Yonge and Dundas area. These developments are producing numerous social, commercial, academic, and aesthetic benefits and opportunities for residents and visitors alike.

One organization in Toronto that is playing an active, dynamic, and exemplary role in all this is Artscape. This remarkable organization has become well-known in arts communities throughout the world for the pioneering work it is doing in urban renewal and revitalization, as well as the creation of captivating and exciting cultural hubs in different locations in the city. This results from bringing artists, animators, and other creative people together with developers, planners, and citizens to create places and spaces that engage citizens fully and actively in the planning and development process and are designed to meet the needs and interests of people and community groups and not just developers, planners, and corporations.

Commencing with its inventive initiative with Artscape Wychwood Barns, this valuable institution has been instrumental in creating and contributing to the development of several other key cultural hubs in strategic parts of this city, such as Artscape West Queen West, Artscape Youngplace, Gibraltar Point, Weston Commons, and Parkdale Arts and Cultural Centre. These hubs are building bridges and creating links and connections among many different artistic, social, industrial, developers,' and citizens' coalitions and constituencies. This work is being enhanced and reinforced by major collaborations between Artscape and the Daniels Corporation, which has also been extremely active in Toronto for many years in creating and building condominiums intimately connected to the arts and culture, including the redevelopment of Regent

Park in conjunction with Toronto Community Housing and the extremely popular and innovative Artscape and Daniels Spectrum and Launchpad initiatives.

These and other developments have put Toronto on the international map as one of the most interesting, stimulating, and enjoyable cities in the world in which to live and work. Over the last several decades and especially over the last few years, Toronto has been recognized as one of the most livable cities in the world—if not *the* most livable—by the United Nations, *The Economist* Intelligence Unit, *Metropolis* magazine, Mercer's Quality of Life Ranking, and others. These rankings are based on a variety of criteria, such as safety, security, education, health care, the environment, the arts, recreation, political stability, walkability, preservation of heritage sites, and others.

Toronto was also ranked as "the best city in the world for youth" in a recent survey commissioned by the New York-based Citi Foundation. This survey delved deeply into employment and growth statistics in addition to the strength of government programs, educational institutions, and entrepreneurial opportunities for people in the 18-to-25 age category. It revealed that Toronto was the most effective city in the world in terms of providing jobs, business opportunities, and entrepreneurial possibilities for young people. This is one of the most pressing requirements in Canada and the world today, due primarily to the high rate of occupational turnover and unemployment, as well as underemployment and precarious and contract employment among youth.

Similar developments to those taking place in Toronto are also occurring in other Canadian cities, such as Montreal, Vancouver, and Calgary, which also rank high on international ratings and rankings. Montreal, for instance, is quickly acquiring a reputation as one of the most attractive and enjoyable cities in the world in which to live and work as well as to visit, due largely to the development of the Quartier des Spectacles that includes La Vitrine, Place des Arts, Musée d'art contemporain de Montréal, as well as equally important developments in Old Montreal such as the well-known Notre Dame Basilica, Montreal Museum of Archaeology and History, Centre d'histoire de Montréal, Arsenal Contemporary Arts, and, more recently, the Cité Mémoire, which enables residents and tourists alike to journey through time by means of the project's after-dark tableaux. This complements such cherished institutions and landmarks in Montreal as the McCord Museum, the Canadian Centre for Architecture, Sainte Catherine Street, Galeria MX, and the Montreal Arts Council, which is one of the oldest and most successful and dynamic municipal arts councils in Canada and the world.

In recent years, these developments have been enhanced by the creation of a great deal of street art and numerous murals, thereby contributing to the aesthetic appeal, character, and charm of Montreal. Particularly important in this regard are developments by such organizations as Être Avec Toi (Ê.A.T), which is composed of a "who's who" of famous graffiti and street artists from Montreal and many other parts of the world, as well as MASSIVart Mural Festival, which is concerned largely with painting murals on the sides of buildings and other notable structures. Due to developments like these, and others, Montreal was the first Canadian city to be added to Google's street-art gallery with more than 150 major murals in place, thus contributing to Montreal's rapidly evolving reputation as an "artistic city" of major importance and considerable stature in the world.

And this is not all. Many developments like these in Toronto, Montreal, and in other Canadian cities such as Vancouver and Calgary have been and are being activated and assisted by the Creative City Network of Canada (CCNC). This not-for-profit, non-governmental service organization was created in 2002 and has become well known internationally for its work as a "national network to facilitate innovation and creativity in municipal structures." It was designed from the outset "to support cultural development by sharing knowledge between municipalities through cultural summits and other means," as well as "to enhance social, economic, and environmental sustainability through collaboration, creativity, innovation, advocacy, inclusiveness, respect, and excellence."

What is true for Canada and Canadian cities is also true for the United States and Europe and for American and European cities. In the United States, for example, most of the largest cities are known for their outstanding artistic accomplishments and developments, including Los Angeles, New York, Boston, Chicago, and many others. Developments in these large cities have been joined by fascinating initiatives in other large cities over the last few decades. An excellent example of this is Philadelphia, which created its Avenue of the Arts on South Broad Street in the 1990s. This development was initiated by a group of local businesspeople, overseen by a dynamic and innovative mayor, and linked together the Academy of Music, the Philadelphia Orchestra, and other important theatrical and musical venues and institutions in the area. As the mayor of Philadelphia at the time, Ed Rendell, stated, "We couldn't have done this without our Avenue of the Arts. It was the first big project, the catalyst for everything.... If we could do this, it would be brilliant. It would revitalize downtown, bring investment downtown and, most importantly, bring *people* downtown—first to visit, and eventually to live."[14] In the years since, this has become true not only of Philadelphia but also of many other cities in the United States, such as Pittsburgh, New Orleans, Tucson, Fort Worth, Santa Fe, Asheville, and others; more than ninety cities have planned, created, or implemented "hubs and districts" in key locations that have stimulated an incredible amount of artistic, commercial, entrepreneurial, and tourist activity.

The same holds true for Europe and European cities as the principal leaders in this field. Ever since Mélina Mercouri, Minister of Culture in Greece, and Jack Lang, Minister of Culture in France, came up with the idea of "cultural capitals" and "cities of culture" devoted to the development of the arts—first broadly defined in 1985—this idea has spread like wildfire throughout Europe and many other parts of the world. In Europe, this initiative started with the designation of one "cultural capital" or "city of culture" each year (the choice was Athens in the first year), but has been expanded since 2007 as a result of its popularity to the naming of two cultural capitals or cities of culture each year. For instance, Rijeka in Croatia and Galway in Ireland are the two cultural capitals or cities of culture in 2020. As these two examples indicate, this project is no longer confined to large cities as it was in the early years, but now encompasses many smaller cities where outstanding artistic and cultural developments have been achieved, such as Porto, Subiu, Liverpool, Vilnus, Pécs, Umeå, Plovdiv, Košice, Bruges, and many others. These developments have been accelerated and intensified by the creation of the organization United Cities and Local Governments (UCLG) and its Culture 21 committee, as well as the development of the Intercultural Cities Index

(ICC), an instrument that measures the level of achievement of intercultural policy implementation in a city and its progress over time, and that compares it with other cities in the world. The goal is to strengthen and enhance the role of the arts and culture in sustainable urban developments as well as enhance urban development in societies as a whole.

Given all the multifarious contributions the arts make in all their aspects to cities—many of them located at the heart and soul of what urban development is really all about—the role of the arts in the development of cities must be seen in a totally new light. Rather than viewing the arts and culture as an afterthought or "the icing on the cake"—as has traditionally been the case—the arts must be seen as the *centrepiece* and *spearhead* that is required to propel communities, towns, and cities to higher levels of accomplishment. This is particularly important for governments, corporations, politicians, and corporate leaders to realize, as they tend to see the challenge confronting urban development as one of squeezing all the available economic, commercial, financial, and tourist potential out of the arts while providing little in return.

Consistent with contemporary experiences in urban development around the world and recent research, it is imperative to recognize that there is an interactive and reinforcing—rather than unilateral and parasitical—relationship between the arts and cities. The arts energize and enrich cities. In return, cities broaden, deepen, and intensify developments in the arts. Both the arts and cities reap the profuse benefits and multiplicity of advantages that emanate from this.

Recognition of this fact should open the doors to a dramatic expansion in funding for the arts at the municipal level. This funding should come from all levels of government—federal, provincial, regional, state, and municipal—as well as from corporations, foundations, and private benefactors. While funding from building programs, infrastructure projects, partnership agreements, and special reserves is important, funding should come primarily from annual appropriations and general revenue. *And it should be used for operating purposes and not only capital projects.* Funding that produces capital infrastructure but does not provide for ongoing artistic performances and activities will never do the job.

A great deal of "strategic rethinking" is necessary here. Rather than viewing funding of the arts as an *expenditure* that has to be endured, it should be seen and treated as an *investment* that has to be embraced. It is an investment that should be designed to produce multiple, cumulative, and long-term benefits and creative outcomes, as well as elicit and induce new opportunities. Funding that produces clustering and integrative effects and ignites other possibilities—such as funding for urban revitalization and renewal, the creation of downtown and suburban cores, hubs, and districts, the stimulation of new experimental and experiential works, the training of skilled personnel—and that provides opportunities for artists and arts organizations to play a major role in urban planning, policy, and decision-making is imperative if the objective is to inject vim, vigor, and vitality into the development of communities, towns, and cities in all parts of the world.

Arts animators and administrators capable of generating new possibilities, initiating change, and engaging large numbers of people in the artistic process have a particularly important role to play in this. There is simply no substitute for well-trained people who are skilled at getting citizens involved in the artistic process and stimulating other opportunities. As

Charles Landry, one of the world's leading authorities on the development of creative cities, contends:

> [W]ealth in cities is created less by what we produce and more by how we use our brains and add value through knowledge and imagination. Cities now have one crucial resource—their people. Human cleverness and creativity are replacing location, natural resources and market access as urban assets. We need to provide the conditions to unleash this imagination.[15]

This initiative is not limited to colossal cities such as New York, London, Paris, Beijing, Tokyo, Rio de Janeiro, Singapore, or Berlin. It is also true for smaller towns, cities, and other forms of urban agglomeration and concentration. Just as contemporary research is revealing that the arts possess numerous clustering, integrative, and triggering capabilities and effects, so it is confirming that many smaller towns and cities are ideal places to live and work because they possess many more high quality artistic institutions and exciting cultural possibilities than they did in the past. Regardless of where one decides to live, work, and thrive, however, one thing is certain. Without the arts securely fastened to the masthead of urban development, life in towns and cities of all shapes, sizes, and types will fall far short of the mark. Presumably this is why Lewis Mumford said that cities are humanity's "greatest work of art." And what is true for cities will also be true for neighbourhoods, communities, towns, and other forms of urban concentration and development in the future.

Chapter 6
The Arts in Turbulent Times

Like people everywhere in the world, artists and arts organizations were shocked and saddened by the terrorist attacks on the World Trade Center and Pentagon on September 11, 2001. The profuse outpouring of grief and anguish that came from actors, musicians, singers, dancers, painters, and playwrights following these tragic and despicable events stands as vivid testimony to this.

As time passed, it became apparent that these were not isolated events, but rather manifestations of something much more serious and disturbing in the world. There was a great deal of anger, hostility, and resentment in many parts of the world. This was confirmed not only by the terrorist attacks on the World Trade Center and Pentagon, but also by violent reactions to globalization, capitalism, huge disparities in income and wealth, famine, poverty, hunger, and deep divisions between different races, religions, cultures, and civilizations.

In 2020 this occurred once again with the COVID-19 pandemic, which has already claimed countless more lives but in a very different way. Not only have all countries, people, and the world as a whole been affected by the coronavirus in one form or another, but once again there is a profuse outpouring of grief, anguish, and emotions by artists and arts organizations. Many have lost their jobs and sources of income, and had their exhibitions and performances cancelled due to severe but necessary restrictions by governments with respect to physical contact in large and small crowds as well as at major gatherings and public and private events.

Undeterred by the gravity of their situation, artists and arts organizations around the world have responded by giving freely of themselves and turning to contemporary communication technologies to create or find new ways to perform or exhibit in groups while being trapped and isolated in their own homes. They have risen to the occasion once again because they want to help millions of people cope with this dreadful disease and find the courage, persistence, and endurance to prevail despite the extent and severity of this worldwide crisis.

Matters worsened considerably later in 2020 when George Floyd, an African American, was killed by police on May 25 in Minneapolis, Minnesota. Almost immediately, protests broke out in that city, across the United States, and around the world as activist organizations such as Black Lives Matter, people of colour, Indigenous groups, and oppressed minorities rebelled against decades and indeed centuries of violence, prejudice, oppression, racism, brutality, and murder, as well as lack of accountability on the part of police and other institutions. With the support of millions of people throughout the world, the protests were transformed into a much broader movement aimed at bringing an end to systemic racism and violence against racialized persons, as well as making significant changes in police budgets and calling for equitable treatment for marginalized people in courts of law and educational institutions and representation on the boards of powerful corporations and in municipal, regional, and national governments. While it is difficult to say what impact these protests and movements will have on the world in the future, one thing is certain. There is no turning back. Much more progress will have to be made in this area in the years ahead if the world is to become a safer, more equitable, and better place.

Obviously fundamental changes are required in the world to deal with these and other debilitating and dangerous problems that have arisen in recent years, including climate change and other environmental crises, vast inequalities in incomes and wealth, the intermingling of millions of people and populations with different and sometimes clashing worldviews, values, customs, traditions, and ways of life, and the perpetual threat of nuclear, chemical, or biological warfare. Indeed, it would not be far off the mark to say that a new world system is needed to deal with such challenges. It is against this backdrop that the arts community must frame and fashion its short- and long-term responses to current events.

The most pressing need of all is to provide people with peaceful and cooperative—rather than violent and confrontational—ways to express their pent-up feelings, emotions, and frustrations. Fortunately, the arts largely do this, although there are times when art must be provocative to challenge the status quo and hold up a mirror to society, encouraging people to make change in constructive rather than destructive fashion. Great Britain realized the importance of this during the Second World War when it created the Arts Council of Great Britain, now Arts Council England. Numerous developments and initiatives like this are needed everywhere in the world today. It is a time to refresh our connection and renew our acquaintance with Beethoven's monumental *Ninth Symphony*, Louis Armstrong's *What a Wonderful World,* Picasso's *Guernica*, Reynaldo Hahn's *Ah Chloris*, Rodger and Hammerstein's *You'll Never Walk Alone*, Lennon's *Imagine*, He Zhanhao and Chen Gang's *The Butterfly Lovers' Violin Concerto*, and Mendelssohn's *Grant Us Peace*, to cite only a few examples of many.

We need a massive build-up of the arts in countries and

communities all over the world. Political, corporate, and educational leaders must be convinced that the arts have a central rather than marginal role to play in the development of societies, countries, and international relations. While military leaders are vying for more money to spend on weapons of war, artistic leaders must demand more money to spend on the arts as vehicles of peace, tolerance, and cooperation, much as Federico Mayor did years ago when he created the Foundation for Peace in Spain.

Expanding the arts in this way will go a long way toward cooling off the world rather than heating it up. It will also go a long way toward building strong foundations and friendly relations among all the diverse peoples, religions, races, countries, and cultures of the world. The distinguished authority on international relations, Paul Braisted, recognized the importance of this when he said:

> Anyone who discards the possibility of developing more friendly relations among people should ponder the alternative long and well. The only alternative is continuing and deepening conflict, with its dangers of increasing reliance upon violence, and the corrosive effects upon human life of distrust and fear.[16]

It will be impossible to prevent such an outcome and instead build strong and friendly relations between people and countries—all people and all countries, not just some people and some countries—without a quantum leap forward in international relations in general and international artistic relations in particular. This is yet another area where the arts can play a crucial role, even if it is a longer-term and more slowly evolving one. As the purveyors of some of humanity's most human and humane expressions, music, dance, drama, literature, and painting expose the real hearts and souls of people and nations. These activities communicate effectively across racial, ethnic, and linguistic divides, geographical boundaries, and political interests, in profound, cooperative, and compelling ways. They reveal most clearly what people and countries are all about, how they have evolved over time, and what they hold most precious and dear to themselves.

This is not the only reason for advocating a massive build-up in international artistic relations. When economic, commercial, and military relations are in flux, as they are today in many parts of the world, international artistic relations provide a strong stabilizing force and calming influence. They cushion the shocks that can easily result from erratic swings in the pendulums of economic, political, commercial, financial, and military power. Thus, a comprehensive program of international artistic relations involving singers, dancers, actors, composers, painters, playwrights, theatre and dance companies, symphony orchestras, choirs, and so forth can provide the glue that is necessary to hold people, races, ethnic groups, countries, and continents together when other forces are operating to divide them. In this way, peace, harmony, happiness, civility, and security—yes, security—are more readily achieved and maintained in the world.

Equally important is the fact that international artistic relations do more than anything else to eradicate fear and suspicion—the kind of fear and suspicion that results from the inability to understand the signs, symbols, customs, traditions, and beliefs of other people and cultures. Through a dramatic expansion in international relations in this area—relations based on in-depth encounters with the artistic achievements of all people and all countries—there is an opportunity to bring all the people and countries of the world into intimate contact. It is an opportunity that is far too important to the future of humanity and the world to pass up. This is yet another area where the arts community has a valuable role to play, not only in turbulent times but in all times.

While political and corporate leaders tend to resist or downplay the importance of the arts and international artistic relations, they are of utmost importance to the world of the future. As developments in the past have repeatedly demonstrated—and demonstrated convincingly—there is an appalling lack of understanding of the different countries, cultures, and civilizations of the world. Without a great deal more emphasis on the arts and international artistic relations, "the clash of cultures and civilizations" is inevitable and could easily become a self-fulfilling prophecy.

The world of the future will obviously be characterized by a great deal more intercultural and interracial mixing, interaction, and borrowing than there is today. Demographic, social, economic, and technological changes will see to this, as will advances in communication, globalization, and computerization. People everywhere will have to learn much more about cultures other than their own if they want to function effectively in the world and live creative, constructive, safe, and fulfilling lives.

As the gateway to cultures and civilizations, the arts have an indispensable role to play. While it is essential to train young people and future generations for careers in the arts and to educate people to participate actively in the arts, it is equally essential to broaden and deepen people's knowledge and understanding of their own culture as well as the cultures of others. The arts do so by exposing people to artistic works, signs, symbols, values, and ideals that are different from their own, as well as by acquainting them with all the diverse cultures and civilizations that exist throughout the world.

At a time when people from all walks of life and all occupations and professions are staking claims to the type of world system that is most needed in the future, the arts community must make a strong case for a world system based on the highest, wisest, and most enduring values and ideals that are embodied in culture and the arts. Included among these values and ideals are the quest for equality, justice, freedom, truth, and peace; the love of beauty, knowledge, and wisdom; the necessity of stability, security, diversity, and cooperation; the importance of caring, sharing, and compassion; the recognition of the needs and rights of others; and the quest for the sublime. Let's not fall into the trap identified by Oscar Wilde many years ago when he declared it is possible to know "the price of everything and the value of nothing."

If a world system based on such values is to be realized, the arts community will have to play a forceful, proactive, and leadership role in all this. This was recognized by James Feibleman when he said:

> There is a sense in which the whole of human culture is a struggle towards the higher values. Can there be any greater human expression of culture than art? Art surely lifts us up, although it would not be likely to exist without us....We were meant to actualize the higher values, and incidental to this task is the privilege of enjoying them.[17]

A world system based on the values embodied in culture and the arts would be an exciting system indeed. It would confirm the fact that the honest expression of feelings and emotions, artistic creation, scientific discovery, lifelong learning, spirituality, friendship, and human love are the most essential things in life—the things that are remembered and cherished long after everything else is forgotten. Not only do they bring genuine fulfillment and happiness, but also they promote peace and harmony rather than conflict and confrontation. Given the state of the world at present and the prospects for the future, it is difficult to see how it will be possible for people and countries in all parts of the world to live in times as volatile and turbulent as these without adopting such a perspective.

Chapter 7
Culture: Beacon of the Future

Profound changes are taking place in the cultural complexion of the world. Not only is the world being transformed as a result of concerns about and protests against racism and inequality as well as medical and public health emergencies, but countless environmental, economic, political, technological, social, and demographic developments are also transforming the world we live in.

If we are to be successful in coming to grips with these challenges, much will depend on our ability to assess the present situation and interpret it correctly. A misreading of the reality with which we are confronted is bound to have serious implications and consequences for the future. In that light, surely one of the biggest questions facing the world today is: Have we learned enough from the COVID-19 pandemic, the anti-racism protests, and other recent events to ensure that such problems and issues can be resolved successfully? And even after these problems are addressed, there is still the environmental crisis to come to grips with and overcome. While the environmental movement has existed for some time—the first Earth Day was celebrated in 1970, and scientists first began to gather evidence of global warming in the 1950s and '60s—recent reports by the UN International Panel on Climate Change and other scientific organizations and environmental agencies show that humanity is losing the battle against climate change and other environmental threats. Not only is the natural environment being polluted, contaminated, and devastated at a rapid rate, but the world's resources are also being utilized at an alarming pace. Clearly major changes in human behaviour and a whole new set of sustainable policies and practices will have to be put in place if the environmental crisis is to be dealt with effectively and the globe's fragile ecosystems are to be protected successfully.

New environmental policies and practices are mandatory in a world characterized by ongoing population growth. Even the most optimistic forecasts suggest that expanding numbers, especially when they are etched against reductions in the amount of arable land and depletion of natural resources, may prove to be one of the most difficult challenges of all. While urbanization offers a temporary reprieve in a purely spatial sense—largely by sanctioning vertical as opposed to horizontal expansion and squeezing more and more people into the same geographical area—it does so at an exorbitant price. Not only does it dramatically increase the amount of air, water, noise, and traffic pollution, but also it makes it more difficult to sustain the level of social, recreational, environmental, and medical amenities that are necessary for a healthy existence.

It would be foolhardy to underestimate the impact that contemporary developments in technology are having and will have on this situation. Not only are they transforming employment, consumer, manufacturing, and many other practices in all parts of the world, but the rapid growth of artificial intelligence, robotics, genetic engineering, and biotechnology promise even more change in everyday procedures and practices in every aspect of life throughout the world.

Technology is clearly a double-edged sword. On the one hand, it opens up vast opportunities for the storage, retrieval, and utilization of knowledge, information, and ideas in every field of human endeavour. On the other hand, it makes it difficult for people to handle the demands and dictates of a technologically oriented and media-dominated world. While the cruelties of war, famine, poverty, human rights abuses, corruption, and the spread of infectious diseases are never easy to confront, they are much more difficult to cope with when news of them is catapulted around the world every second of every day. Without doubt, it will take a great deal of psychic endurance and mental toughness on the part of all people and all countries to deal with the profundity and propinquity of such matters.

Placed alongside all the problems posed by technological change are the demographic and social developments taking place in the world. Not only have the populations of most countries become much more pluralistic and multicultural in character—thereby increasing the potential for racial violence and ethnic unrest—but there are also all the changes going on in the way people interact with each other as a result of social media and internet organizations like Facebook, Twitter, Google, and many others. There are also conflicts among people of different genders and ethnicities. These developments are occurring at a time when many of the traditional safeguards and support systems that had been created to cushion the shock of unprecedented and unpredictable social change are undergoing profound transformations of their own or even breaking down. Whereas it was once possible to look to the family, church, temple, synagogue, mosque, neighbourhood, or community to cushion the shocks of unprecedented social dislocations and change, this seems much more unlikely if not impossible for many people today.

Contemporary developments in politics are also having a powerful effect on this situation. There is hardly a country anywhere in the world today that is not experiencing fundamental shifts in its political ideologies, geographical borders, bureaucratic practices, and governmental procedures.

Closely connected to these political changes are many economic changes. The financial catastrophe caused by COVID-19 and the shift from free trade to protectionism in some parts of the world (such as the United States) have brought with them countless developments in both the public and private sector, as well as greater concentrations of wealth and power in fewer hands, erratic fluctuations in stock markets, the division of the world into ever larger trading blocks and "superstates" such as the United States, China, and Russia, and still other problems. While some countries have been more fortunate than others in weathering these cataclysmic changes and major transformations, few have managed to escape the consequences of radically changed methods of production and distribution, altered forms of employment and expenditure, rapid escalations in public and private debt, and a great deal else. A new economic reality is taking hold in the world—a reality that suggests that the days of continuous economic growth and increased affluence are over and the days of austerity, consolidation, and thrift have set in. One need only look at the lengthening lists of welfare recipients, the proliferation of food banks, and the growing ranks of the unemployed, underemployed, and precariously and contractually employed to confirm this.

There is one other development taking place in the world that should also be addressed here—people's reactions to capitalism, globalization, the emergence of larger and larger trading blocks, and the concentration of financial, commercial, technological, and media power in ever fewer hands.

There can be little doubt that such developments are having a destabilizing and disorienting effect on people and countries in all parts of the world. This is manifesting itself in a number of countervailing measures and movements that aim to increase people's sense of empowerment and control over the decision-making processes affecting their lives. Whether it is the quest for independence, identity, sovereignty, or solidarity, or the resurfacing of interest in neighbourhoods and communities, the consequences are the same. The more pressure is exerted toward globalization and other international developments, the more people initiate and institute countervailing movements, projects, and measures aimed at taking greater control over their destinies and lives.

When all these many different developments are placed side by side and added up, they produce a portrait of a world that is in a state of rapid if not revolutionary change. What is most distinctive about this world is not only its lack of certainty, security, and order, but also its fluidity and vulnerability. Not only are events happening at lightning speed, but they are intimately and inexorably interconnected.

Given this situation, it is easy to understand why more and more people in the world are feeling frightened, disoriented, confused, and insecure. It is not that all of these changes are negative. In fact, some of them, such as the quest for equality and the environmental movement, are very positive. It is simply that they are occurring at such an accelerated and unprecedented rate, and are so pervasive and powerful in their size, scope, impact, and influence, that they are making it difficult for people to know how to respond. In fact, change itself has become a monumental problem in the modern world. It has become so rapid, complex, volatile, and pronounced that people in many parts of the world are having the utmost difficulty coping with it, and it threatens to escalate out of control.

What seems to be lurking behind all these changes is the growing realization that a matrix of problems has emerged throughout the world that stands well beyond the global system that has been designed to deal with them. Whether it is the medical and environmental situation, huge disparities and inequalities in income and wealth, the breakdown of social systems, the erosion of ethical and spiritual values, or ethnic, racial, and gender unrest, there is a sinking feeling among most leaders and many citizens everywhere in the world that the global system itself could be on the verge of collapse. It is not only economic policies, political ideologies, social conventions, and environmental practices that are being severely tested. More essentially and fundamentally, it is the entire system of theory and practice that humanity has built up over the last few centuries to provide order, stability, security, and progress in the world, as well as to deliver higher standards of living and a better quality of life for more people and countries, that is being shaken to its very foundations.

It is within this rapidly evolving world situation that culture is emerging as a powerful and dynamic force in the world. This is manifesting itself in a number of developments that have occurred over the last few decades. For the aforementioned changes are not isolated and disconnected events. On the contrary, they are connected, inevitable, and a fundamental dimension of the response to the numerous municipal, regional, national, and international transformations that are going on in all parts of the world today and typify contemporary times. Clearly culture contains within itself the potential and means that are needed to address many of the most debilitating and complex problems confronting humanity and the world at present as well as in the future. Seen from this perspective, there is a great deal of truth in Victor Hugo's shrewd observation that "*greater than the tread of mighty armies is an idea whose time has come.*" For culture is surely an idea whose time has not only come but now must be fully realized.

What is it about culture that makes it indispensable to the world of the present and the future? Four things. First, the ability to provide a holistic perspective on the world and the most important things in the world and in life. Second, the capacity to yield worldviews, values, value systems, lifestyles, and so forth that are more humane, enlightened, and in tune with the newly emerging global reality. Third, the ability to interpret history in a more accurate and authentic way. And fourth, the capacity to come to grips with the world's most difficult, demanding, and life-threatening problems, as well as to provide a more effective theoretical and practical system for dealing with these problems and carrying humanity forward into a new age.

Many may argue that the ability to provide a holistic perspective on the world may be helpful, but not really all that necessary in terms of addressing the debilitating and dangerous problems confronting humanity. However when Fritjof Capra claimed that "all the difficult economic, environmental, social, political and human problems of our times are really different facets of one and the same crisis, and that crisis is essentially a crisis in perception," he put his finger on the crux of this matter.[18] For he underlined the crucial importance of "the art of seeing" as a necessary requirement for effective problem solving. Perhaps this is why Goethe observed towards the end of his life that "it was with the eye more than with all the other organs that I learned to comprehend the world."[19]

Alexander King of the Club of Rome went even further in this respect. In an essay underlining the dire need for a multidisciplinary or holistic rather than specialized and partial perspective on contemporary problems and problem-solving he said:

> Nearly all contemporary social problems, whether national or global, are interrelated and exceedingly complex, a tangled mass of individual threads connected in ways which are only dimly understood, so that attempts to solve a specific issue have repercussions on many others. Furthermore, each problem has many elements, technical, economic, social, political and human and can seldom be resolved by the politician, scientist, engineer or economist in isolation. With the increasing interdependence of nations and the emergence of so many problems of global dimension, many disciplines have to be called simultaneously into play. Yet multidisciplinary action is difficult to achieve, for society is organized essentially on a vertical basis. Government departments are grouped by sector, and the policies of each are devised with only secondary consideration of their effects on the policies of the others. The same may be said of the universities, organized by faculty, department and sub-department, each deepening understanding of its particular specialization and usually unfamiliar with the others' findings.[20]

What is becoming increasingly apparent is that the disadvantages of specialization outweigh the advantages, despite the incredible importance of specialization in all disciplines and fields of human endeavour. Nevertheless, piling more and more areas of specialization on top of each other will no longer work, because specialization itself has become the problem. While we know a great deal about disciplines and activities in their own right, as Alexander King pointed out, we know very little about the complex relationships that exist—or do not exist—between and among them. When economists tell us we must consume more because this is essential for economic growth and environmentalists tell us we must consume less because this is imperative to come to grips with climate change, no amount of discussion between economists and environmentalists will resolve this contradiction. Obviously, a new way of seeing and understanding is imperative, one that enables us to see both the economy *and* the environment from a holistic or all-encompassing perspective.

Culture provides this perspective. Defined in holistic terms as a "complex whole" or "total way of life" in the way that most anthropologists and cultural historians do, culture focuses not only on the whole, but also on the complex relationships that comprise the whole.[21]

Of all the various relationships that in combination constitute the holistic perspective provided by culture, three in particular stand head and shoulders above the rest. They deserve attention because they are so fundamentally related to the human condition, the environmental crisis, sustainable development, and the survival and well-being of all the diverse species in the world. These three relationships are the relationship of people and countries in and of themselves as well as to each other; their relationship to the many different things they create; and their relationship to the natural environment.

The relationship of people and countries in and of themselves and to each other is intimately related to people's individual and collective behavior, actions, welfare, and well-being. The relationship of people to the many different things they create is closely linked to people's and countries' material and non-material development. And finally, and surely most importantly of all at this particular stage in global development and human affairs, the relationship of people and countries to the natural environment is inexorably connected to the ecological association they have with nature and all the forms of plant and animal life that exist throughout the world.

It is reassuring to know that increasing numbers of people, organizations, and countries in the world are realizing that culture as it is perceived and understood today includes much more than the arts, humanities, and the mass media or "cultural industries," essential as these activities and areas are. In fact, when today we talk about people being "the products of their culture," this means they are not only products of the arts, humanities, and the mass media or cultural industries but also products of economic systems, political ideologies, social conventions, educational experiences, communications practices, religious beliefs, environmental circumstances, and a great deal more. In other words, they are the products of everything they do, create, produce, and consume, as well as the way they live their lives, position themselves in the world, and behave and act in the world. This fundamental shift in perceptual thinking concerning the orbit and purview of culture was confirmed by the member states of UNESCO when they unanimously endorsed the following definition of culture at the second World Conference on Cultural Policy in Mexico City in 1982:

> Culture ought to be considered today the whole collection of distinctive traits, spiritual and material, intellectual

> and affective, which characterize a society or social group. It comprises, besides arts and letters, modes of life, human rights, value systems, traditions and beliefs.[22]

The arguments for adopting this all-encompassing and much more compelling perception and understanding of culture were set out even more forcefully in the planning documents and working papers for the World Decade for Cultural Development from 1989 to 1997.

> Reflection on the subject of cultural development finally led to what was almost a new definition of culture by the participants at the Mexico City Conference. Without neglecting the importance of creativity as expressed in intellectual and artistic activity, they considered it important to broaden the notion of culture to include behaviour patterns and individuals' view of themselves, of society, and of the outside world. In this perspective, the cultural life of a society may be seen to express itself through its way of living and being, through its perceptions and self-perceptions, its behaviour patterns, values and beliefs.
>
> Where development action is concerned, the implications of such a conception of culture are evident: any project which fails to take into account both the natural and cultural environment of a given population runs the risk of failure. In this statement lie the roots of the strategy proposed by the participants in the Mexico Conference in the context of the World Decade for Cultural Development. This strategy implies a series of coordinated actions designed to restore cultural and

> human values to their central place in economic and technological development.[23]

Armed with this holistic, all-encompassing understanding of culture, we are in a perfect position to recognize how culture can be helpful in transforming notions about development, worldviews, values, value systems, lifestyles, individual and collective behaviour, customs, traditions, beliefs, and a great deal else.

Adoption of this holistic perception of culture enables us to transform our understanding of the real nature and meaning of development in general and sustainable development in particular. Regardless of whether it is neighbourhoods, communities, towns, cities, regions, countries, or the world as a whole being considered or discussed, development is no longer a one-sided, partial, or partisan affair based largely on economic, technological, political, commercial, and financial activities. On the contrary, it is an all-inclusive, integrative, and comprehensive affair based on a judicious blending of all the determinants of development: economic, social, political, environmental, artistic, humanistic, technological, scientific, recreational, spiritual, and so forth. It is qualitative as well as quantitative; an art as well as a science; as concerned with things of the heart, the soul, the intellect, and the spirit as it is with money, materialism, power, and the pocketbook.

When development is defined in this all-inclusive and comprehensive way, can any country in the world really claim to be "developed"? On the contrary, are not all countries in various stages of development, struggling to make improvements in *all* the multifarious determinants of development and working diligently to achieve a better balance and harmony between and among these diverse determinants? Surely all countries are common companions on the road to sustainable development in this sense; they are merely taking different routes and paths depending on their cultures, values, and needs. Some may have reasonably well-developed economic and technological resources while their artistic, social, and spiritual resources require improvement. Others may have more developed aesthetic, social, or spiritual resources but their economic and technological resources require improvement. The point is, however, that all countries are in a similar developmental boat.

What we must break away from is the idea that some countries are "developed" and others are not, since all this has produced is a world that is divided into many different and unequal parts, as well as a world order that has produced some of the worst abuses and injustices in human history. Clearly, what we must work towards is an understanding that development—like culture—is an evolutionary and all-encompassing affair as well as a dynamic and organic process that is constantly changing, evolving, mutating, and adapting over time in response to new conditions and altered circumstances. For what is the point of development if it is not to make improvements in *all* the various components and dimensions of the human condition and global situation.

More enlightened and engaging worldviews, values, value systems, lifestyles, and modes of behaviour are certain to flow from this balanced and more all-embracing and harmonious understanding of development. These worldviews, values, value systems, life styles, and modes of behaviour should remind us that the real challenge in life and in the world is to live a good, upright, and meaningful life, not in the contemporary sense of a life filled with *excessive* rather than *responsible* consumer and consumption practices, but on the contrary in the classical sense of a life defined by high ethical standards, spiritual fulfillment, intellectual integrity, and captivating ideals. This confirms that the honest sharing of feelings and emotions, artistic creation, lifelong learning, scientific discovery, sharing, caring, compassion, friendships, and human love are, as mentioned earlier, still the most important things in life, the things that are remembered long after everything else is forgotten. Not only does a focus on these things reduce the drain and strain on natural resources, thereby holding the key to the environmental crisis that is engulfing the globe at present, but they are also the things that bring real joy, happiness, fulfillment, and contentment in life, thereby solving the "riddle of maldevelopment."

As these worldviews, values, value systems, lifestyles, and modes of behaviour gather momentum and take hold in the world, they are sure to produce more compatible and harmonious associations with nature, ones based on unity with nature rather than supremacy over nature. This should enable humankind to take a much more restrained and common-sense approach to the natural environment. The name of the game in the future should be conservation, renewal, and never taking more from the natural environment than is necessary, rather than exploitation and spoliation. Not only will this enable humanity to treat nature with the dignity, reverence, and respect it so richly deserves, but also it will permit people to enjoy decent *styles of living* without straining global resources and the carrying capacity of the earth to the breaking point.

New worldviews, values, value systems, styles of living, and concepts of development will also help immensely in the complex task of creating more accurate and authentic interpretations of history. While this is exceedingly difficult, as recent encounters with a number of revisionist theories of history have revealed, it simply must be done if we are to arrive at a more impartial and legitimate interpretation of historical evolution and change to carry forward into the future.

In the execution of this task, one objective should transcend all the rest. It is the objective of truth. The world can ill-afford to have major transfers in political power or the retracing of geographical borders and boundaries if they are based on the substitution of one distorted interpretation of history for another. Where interpretations of history are truthful, impartial, and factual, they should prove helpful in confronting and overcoming some of the greatest injustices in the world—injustices that stand in the way of planetary progress in the present and the future.

As matters stand now, major injustices are being done to many Indigenous peoples in the world as well as to many ethnic minorities and racial groups as a result of the one-sided and highly biased accounts of historical development. While some progress has been made in this area in recent years, largely as a result of efforts by the Indigenous peoples themselves as well as specific ethnic and racial groups and several African, Asian and South American nations, the problem will really only be fully eradicated when the contributions that all marginalized, suppressed, and oppressed peoples and groups have made—and are making—to the human condition and world situation are fully recognized and given their due. A cultural interpretation of history provides a way of levelling up the scales of historical justice in this sense, largely by replacing partisan and one-sided renderings of historical developments with a rendering of historical evolution and change that is more accurate, authentic, and in tune with the contributions that all peoples, countries, and cultures have made and are making to the world. In order to be fully effective, however, the cultural interpretation of history in general—and culture in particular—must prove capable of acting as a real "beacon of the future," with the ability to "warn of impending danger" as well as "illuminate a "vital, viable, and safe path to the future" in exactly the same way that all effective beacons do.[24]

And this is not all. When the cultural interpretation of history is combined with more enlightened worldviews, values, value systems, environmental practices, styles of living, and concepts of development, it should open the doors to a new type of age in the future.

What type of age should this be? Certainly not the kind of age where two or three superpowers speak softly (or loudly) and carry a big stick. Nor should it be the kind of homogenized and uniform age that technologists and communication advocates propose. Rather, it should be the kind of age where a prominent place is created for culture at the very centre of individual, community, regional, national, and international development, and the world as a whole is redesigned according to culture's highest, wisest, and more enduring principles, practices, values, and policies.

In the creation of this type of age, a central role should be reserved for the cultural heritage of humankind. In the final analysis, global development and world progress do not consist of the fashioning of individual works, the building up of specific institutions, or the creation of particular countries and culture. Regardless of how important these things are—and there is no intention here of undervaluing their value and importance—they are all means towards a much more enthralling and enduring end, namely the development and diffusion of a universal storehouse of creative cultural achievements by all cultures and countries for appreciation and use by all the world's inhabitants and citizens. As the shining star that is discernible amidst the rise and fall of specific countries and particular cultures, is this jewel in humanity's crown not the true measure of humankind's collective progress down through the ages? Not only is it the product of all peoples and all countries, but also it is the birthright of all citizens, regardless of their educational level, socio-economic circumstances, or geographical location in the world.

Why is it so essential at the present juncture in human history to project this cherished heritage of hope into the foreground rather than permitting it to remain in the background? It is essential because it will not be possible to solve the rapidly-escalating and life-threatening *transnational* problems of modern times—the international spread of infectious diseases, racial and ethnic inequalities, the environmental crisis, escalating violence and terrorism, resource shortages, income inequality and poverty, and the constant threat of a nuclear disaster—without full familiarity with and collective sharing of this universal treasure trove of cultural achievements and creativity. The great Indian sage Rabindranath Tagore foresaw this day when he said "we must prepare the field for the cooperation of all cultures of the world where all will give and take from each other. This is the keynote of the coming age."[25] Ultimately, this is what makes global diffusion and full utilization of the universal cultural heritage of humankind, as well as according a central role to culture in the world, our only real hope for human survival, developmental sustainability, and environmental well-being in the years, decades, and centuries ahead.

Chapter 8
The Case for Culture

Culture, like freedom, is never something
which once gained can be taken for granted;
it is a matter of ceaseless effort.
—Hugh Jenkins[26]

I have worked in the cultural field for more than fifty years. During this time, virtually every person I have met working in this field has felt that culture should play a central role in the world.

This is imperative in view of the present state of the world and prospects for the future. Clearly culture has a crucial role to play in coming to grips with the world's most difficult, dangerous, and debilitating problems, as well as creating more peace, harmony, happiness, and cooperation in the world.

For centuries, the case for culture was made in terms of the arts and treating the arts as "ends in themselves." This was because the arts and culture were deemed to be synonymous and were valued primarily for their intrinsic qualities. This included bringing a great deal of joy, happiness, and hope into people's lives, revealing a great deal about the nature of the world and most things in the world, and inspiring people to reach above and beyond themselves in the search for the sublime. This view of the arts and culture reached its zenith during the Renaissance and the Romantic era, when the arts were accorded a high priority in society because they played an important role in people's lives in both the individual and collective sense.

Things started to change in this respect after the Second

World War when a powerful relationship was created between science, economics, industry, technology, government, and the political process. In the governmental and educational fields, there was a discernible increase in funding for economic, scientific, industrial, and technological activities, programs, and projects and a discernible decrease in funding artistic and humanistic activities, programs, and projects. This occurred first in the western world and then in many other parts of the world as well.

It didn't take long for people in the cultural field to get the message. By the 1970s, it was clear that the traditional case for culture was rapidly losing ground. A new case had to be made—a case capable of producing more funding for culture, which at that time was seen by business, government, foundations, and private benefactors largely in terms of the arts.

By this time, the reasons why this funding was so essential were readily apparent. As William Baumol and William Bowen confirmed in their book *Performing Arts: The Economic Dilemma*, the dependency of the arts on governments and other public and private institutions for funding was not due to artists and arts organizations mismanaging their money, as many people thought, but rather because they experienced a gap between their total expenses and earned income. This was because they were not able to take advantage of technological gains to increase efficiencies and reduce costs in the same way as most industries. As the authors pointed out, it took the same amount of time and number of players to perform a Beethoven symphony when their book was published in 1968—and it still does today!—as it did when Beethoven first composed the symphony more than two centuries earlier. Meanwhile, the costs of performing this symphony had risen dramatically.

While it was important to make the new case for culture to corporations, foundations, educational institutions, and private benefactors, it was especially important to make it to governments. This was because governments were getting much more involved in funding a variety of societal activities and were looking for "hard data" and "concrete arguments" to convince citizens that spending taxpayers' dollars on culture and the arts was justified. It was political and governmental requirements like this—particularly when they were combined with many other developments taking place in the world at the same time—that convinced people in the cultural field that the case for culture had to be made in practical and quantitative terms.

In order to do this, it was necessary to convince governments that culture produced economic, commercial, and financial benefits. As a result, numerous studies were undertaken by people in the cultural field to demonstrate to governments and other public and private institutions that millions of dollars were spent on the arts and culture as a result of the construction of capital facilities, people's attendance at artistic events, and especially expenditures on hotels, restaurants, clothing, transportation, communications, tourism, and a great deal else.

It wasn't long after these studies were completed that culture began to be treated as a component of economics, especially when the new discipline of cultural economics was created to examine cultural issues and problems from an economic perspective. A related development to this took place around the same time. It was the commitment made to proving the arts were not elitist, but, on the contrary, engaged large numbers of people in the artistic process. This resulted in many more studies designed to document the size, composition, and character of arts audiences. These studies proved helpful to governments and other funding agencies in justifying their funding for culture, since they provided factual evidence that arts audiences were much larger and far more diversified than was assumed.

While these studies served a valuable purpose in justifying public and private financial support for culture, they were not without their problems. In order to make the new case for culture, it was necessary to abandon the traditional practice of treating culture as an end in itself and justifying it on the basis of its intrinsic qualities, and instead to start treating culture as a means to other ends, justifying it because of its extrinsic benefits. This set a dangerous precedent, since it meant that culture was no longer valued primarily for what it was, and is, but rather for its ability to satisfy the needs of other institutions, activities, and sectors in society. Most of these needs were concerned with generating economic activity and maximizing economic growth.

This became apparent when the definition of culture was expanded to include "the cultural industries." While most people in business, government, foundations, and so forth were prepared to admit that the arts made a contribution to the economy and the rate of economic growth, most felt this contribution paled in comparison to the contributions made by most other sectors of society. In fact, a strong argument could be made for the fact that governments, corporations, foundations, and international organizations really only got interested in the economic potential of culture after the broadcasting, recording, film, book publishing, and other cultural industries were added to the list. This was because the economic impact generated by these industries was many times greater than that of the arts in their traditional "live" form, because the products of the cultural industries could be mass produced and were not "one of a kind" as most artistic activities are.

Not all people in the cultural field felt the case for culture should be made in economic terms, especially when it didn't deliver the results that many people hoped for and expected. While supporters of the new case for culture claimed that this was the price that had to be paid for generating more public and private support for culture and that it was naïve and simplistic to think otherwise, others felt that additional arguments had be made for culture and not only an economic argument.

One of these arguments was advanced by the Council of Europe in its report *In from the Margins: A Contribution to the Debate on Culture and Development in Europe* published in 1997. As the title suggested, the report was based on the belief that culture should be brought in from the margins and play a more mainstream role in society. According to the authors of this report, this could be achieved most effectively by focusing on the "social contributions of culture," especially bringing people together, sharing experiences, reducing the global cultural gap, mobilizing people and communities, and working in societies in which the mass media and modern communications played an important role. The report was produced by a group of policy-makers, researchers, and arts managers, and, like many reports published at this time, relied heavily on statistics, indicators, and quantitative methods to make its case.

By this time, UNESCO was deeply involved in the quest to establish a new case for culture. Not only was it actively involved in the World Decade for Culture and Development from 1988 to 1997—which was designed to focus on the role that culture plays in development in general and the development of countries in particular—but also it played a prominent role in the World Commission on Culture and Development from 1993 to 1995. This commission, which was headed up by Javier Pérez de Cuéllar, former Secretary General of the United Nations, was committed to examining culture's role in the world and making recommendations concerning its future development. When the commission released its report, *Our Creative Diversity*, in 1996, culture was defined in substantially broader terms than the arts and the cultural industries, and even as "the total way of life of people and countries." As the title of the report implied, a great deal of emphasis was placed on creativity and diversity as two of the most essential elements in culture, and on the key role they play in the world.

As far as creativity was concerned, this was manifested most conspicuously in the work of Richard Florida. He became well-known throughout the world for his research and writing on "the creative class" and the dynamic role it played in urban development. His books and research on this subject—and especially his book *The Rise of the Creative Class: How It's Transforming Work, Leisure, Community and Everyday Life*—documented the fact that creative people such as artists, designers, architects, activists, inventors, and advertisers were providing the impetus and innovations that were necessary to broaden, deepen, intensify, and enrich developments in urban life. His work was embraced by many people in the arts and cultural field as yet another indication of the economic potential of culture and the role it is capable of playing as a generator and driver of economic activity.

As far as diversity was concerned, it stemmed from a different set of factors and forces. This had to do with the trend that was taking place in the world at that time towards uniformity, and with it, the threat to diversity that was evident in all parts of the world. Spurred on by Canada and France, UNESCO was so concerned about this threat that it created a worldwide movement that led to the signing of the *Convention on the Protection and Promotion of the Diversity of Cultural Expressions* in 2005.

This convention is a legally binding global agreement that ensures that artists, cultural professionals, practitioners, and citizens can create, produce, disseminate, have access to, and enjoy a broad range of cultural goods, services, and activities—***including their own***—in every country and region of the world. It was adopted because of the urgency of establishing and implementing an international agreement that recognized the importance of cultural goods, services, and activities as vehicles of identity, value, and meaning in their own right, and not only as commodities, consumer products, and objects of trade, industry, and commerce.

By the time the UNESCO convention was signed in 2005, climate change, global warming, and the environmental crisis had become major international issues and concerns, as was the need to achieve "sustainable development."

The origins of this idea can be traced back to 1983 when the World Commission on Environment and Development—also known as the Brundtland Commission—was created. The commission's report, *Our Common Future*, was published in 1987. It argued that all future development must be sustainable. In order to achieve this, it was necessary to take the needs and interests of future generations and the natural environment—and not just the needs and interests of the present generation—fully and effectively into account. While it was realized that it would take time to produce the transformation in values, lifestyles, and individual and collective behaviour that was necessary for this, many public and private institutions immediately commenced the search for ways and means to make sustainable development a reality.

One of these ways was deemed to be through the development of "the creative economy." According to the United Nations Conference on Trade and Development (UNCTAD), the creative economy is "an emerging concept that deals with the interface between creativity, culture, economics, and technology in a contemporary world dominated by images, sounds, texts and symbols." What was exciting about this idea for people working in the cultural field was the realization that culture and creativity were intimately connected, could be situated at the core of the creative economy, and seen as "driving forces" in the development of economies of this type. As UNCTAD stated in its *Creative Economy Report* in 2010, "Adequately nurtured, creativity fuels culture, infuses a human-centred development, and constitutes the key ingredient in job creation, innovation and trade while contributing to social inclusion, cultural diversity and environmental sustainability."

While some people in the cultural field felt that the focus of attention at that time should be on culture's contribution to the "creative economy," others felt it should be on culture's role as "the fourth pillar of sustainable development."

This occurred when the idea of "pillars of sustainable development" surfaced after the report of the Commission on Environment and Development was published and adopted by many people in corporate, governmental, political, and diplomatic communities around the world. While economics was seen and treated as "the first pillar of sustainable development," many people in the environmental field felt that the environment should be seen and treated as "the second pillar of sustainable development," and, as such, given a much higher priority in public policy, planning, and decision-making. Not long after this, pressure was exerted to make social affairs "the third pillar of sustainable development." And then, more recently, culture was added as "the fourth pillar of sustainable development."

Just as Richard Florida played a pivotal role in the development of the concept of the creative class, which led to such notions as the creative sector and the creative economy, so Jon Hawkes played a pivotal role in the development of the concept of culture as the fourth pillar of sustainable development. His book *The Fourth Pillar of Sustainability: Culture's Essential Role in Public Planning* was instrumental in convincing many authorities in business, government, and politics that culture has an important role to play in global development and human affairs. This would not have been possible without a great deal of advocacy and full support from UNESCO, Agenda 21 for Culture, the World Summit on Sustainable Development, and others.

This is where matters stand at present with respect to the case for culture. It is made largely in terms of culture as the arts and the cultural industries, a means to other ends rather than ends in themselves, and valued primarily for their extrinsic rather than intrinsic qualities. It is also being made primarily in terms of culture being a component part of economics and economies, a generator of economic activity, a driver of "the creative economy," and one of the four main pillars of sustainable development. While some people are still making this case in social terms, it pales by comparison to the case made in economic terms.

While these initiatives have played a valuable role in keeping the case for culture up-to-date with most contemporary developments, they tend to reinforce the status quo and existing way of doing things. The problem is that the status quo and existing way of doing things are not sustainable because they are making phenomenal demands on the natural environment, the world's scarce resources, human beings, and the carrying capacity of the earth.

It doesn't take a psychic to depict the kind of world that could result in the near future if this practice is maintained, especially as world population increases, resources are used up, the earth's temperature rises, and the carrying capacity of the planet is approached. Not only will this result in a great deal more environmental exhaustion and degradation, but also it will produce many more rifts and conflicts between the diverse peoples and countries of the world. This explains why there is a growing awareness throughout the world that humanity cannot go on doing things the way they have been done in the past or are being done at present. Things must change—and change substantially—if environmental sustainability and human welfare and well-being are to be assured in the future.

Can culture play a crucial role in this? Surely it can. Not only does culture possess the capacity to bring about the most essential change in the world of all—namely a fundamental transformation in the relationship between human being and the natural environment—but it also possesses the potential to chart a new course for humanity and the world.

In order to do this, two developments are imperative. The first is to take advantage of the all-encompassing holistic definition of culture as a "complex whole" or the "total way of life" of people and countries. The second is to treat culture as an end in itself as well as a means to other ends, thereby valuing it for both its intrinsic and extrinsic qualities.

In combination, these two requirements provide the foundations that are necessary to make a quantum leap in the case for culture. It is a leap based on the belief that culture has a central rather than peripheral role to play in the world. For what these two requirements do is change the *context* within which all developments in the world take place. Not only does this make it possible to change the *contents* of these developments, since context determines contents, but also it makes it possible to realize culture's full potential and ability to play a mainstream rather than marginal role in the world. Surely this is what Léopold Senghor, first president of Senegal and a distinguished poet and cultural scholar, had in mind when he said, "Culture is the alpha and omega of any sound development policy."

Dealing with culture in this all-encompassing, holistic sense is imperative for other reasons as well. Most importantly, it confirms the fact that the world is made up of culture and cultures in this all-inclusive sense at its core and in its fundamental essence, because the whole determines the parts and is greater than the parts and the sum of the parts. This also makes it possible to see the big picture; address crucial problems and strategic relationships in the big picture; facilitate the change that is necessary in people's overall way of life and lifestyles by achieving a better balance between the material and non-material dimensions of development; and focus on the whole rather than a part of the whole. Without these developments, and others, it will not be possible to solve the environmental crisis. Nor will it be possible to achieve sustainable development, realize unity in diversity, and create more peace, harmony, and happiness in the world.

It follows from this that the challenge of the future is to develop culture and cultures in breadth and depth, achieve balance and harmony between and among the many different parts of culture and cultures, and position cultures effectively in the natural, historical, and global environment.

Developing culture in breadth means taking advantage of all the many different ways culture manifests itself in the world, from the artistic and humanistic to the ecological and cosmological. When this occurs, there is very little in the world that is not concerned with culture or affected by culture. This includes all activities engaged in by people—from the artistic and social to the economic, political, and environmental—as well as all citizens, groups, organizations, towns, cities, countries, nature, the natural environment, and other species.

Developing culture in depth means opening up a commanding place for culture's most cherished values and ideals at the heart of development, especially the quest for peace, order, equality, and diversity, the necessity of freedom, migration, justice, and truth, the priceless value of the cultural heritage of humankind, the search for unity, beauty, truth, and the sublime, and others. Could there be anything in the world more important or urgent than this, given the state of the world today and prospects for the future?

Achieving balance and harmony between and among the many different component parts of culture and cultures is equally essential. The cultural historian and scholar Johann Huizinga gave us a profound insight into the necessity of this when, following his assessment of numerous cultures throughout the world, he said "the realities of economic life, of power, of technology, of everything conducive to man's material well-being, must be balanced by strongly developed spiritual, intellectual, moral and aesthetic values."[27] Not only is this the solution to realizing a great deal more well-being and happiness in the world, but also it is the key to establishing the arts as the "gateway" to culture and cultures.

Positioning cultures effectively in the natural, historical, and global environment is equally essential This is necessary to reduce the huge ecological footprint we are imposing on the earth, learn from our mistakes of the past and correct them in the present and the future, come to grips with the cultural baggage we have inherited from previous generations, overcome racism, violence, oppression, prejudice, terrorism, and hate, and interact, share, and connect with other people and cultures on a more human, humane, and compassionate basis.

Many benefits and opportunities will result from this. Most fundamentally, humanity's demands on the natural environment would be substantially reduced because many spiritual, intellectual, moral, and aesthetic activities are labour-intensive rather than material-intensive, and therefore do not make as many demands on the natural environment and resources of nature as most industrial, manufacturing, technological, and commercial activities.

And this is not all. Putting a great deal more emphasis on spiritual, intellectual, moral, and aesthetic activities will produce more caring, sharing, and cooperation in the world. This could have a favourable effect on income distribution throughout the world, activate a major shift away from material and monetary wealth and towards human and spiritual well-being, and help the oppressed and less fortunate peoples and countries of the world.

When culture and cultures are visualized and dealt with in this comprehensive and compelling manner, there is no doubt that culture possesses the potential to play a central role in the world in both the theoretical and practical sense. This means "doing" culture for culture's sake rather than for the sake of economics and economies, as well as treating culture as the centrepiece of the world system and principal preoccupation of municipal, regional, national, and international development. Let's get people and institutions in all parts of the world talking about this and preparing for it. For this is what the case for culture is really all about—ensuring that culture and cultures play a central rather than marginal role in global development and human affairs in the years, decades, and centuries ahead.

Chapter 9

Culture and Cultures: Crucial Learning Requirements

There is mounting evidence to confirm that culture and cultures will play a powerful role in the world of the future. As this occurs, people will have to learn a great deal more about culture and cultures if they want to live creative, constructive, and fulfilling lives, and communities, cities, countries, and the world as a whole are to function effectively.

There are many reasons for this. In the first place, culture and cultures are growing rapidly in importance in all parts of the world today and are destined to play a much more forceful role in the world of the future. Many developments throughout the world confirm this. One is the escalating importance of culture and cultures in individual, institutional, municipal, regional, national, and international affairs, as confirmed in the 1980s and '90s by the creation of the World Decade for Cultural Development and the World Commission on Culture and Development by the United Nations and UNESCO.[28] Another is the increased emphasis accorded to culture and cultures by countries and governments. Whereas culture and cultures were largely ignored at this level three or four decades ago, virtually every country and government in the world today is pursuing measures intended to develop culture and cultures, from passing legislation to protect the heritage of history to executing plans, programs, and policies to increase citizen participation in cultural life. Yet another development is the use of terms such as global culture, corporate culture, media culture, political culture, popular culture, elite culture, social culture, youth culture, economic culture, cyberculture, and environmental culture in public and private discourse. Use of these terms indicates that people are becoming much more "culture conscious," as well as more aware of the important role culture and cultures are playing in the world. A final development, and perhaps the most telling of all, is the establishment of numerous courses, programs, centres, institutes, and chairs in cultural studies in post-secondary educational institutions throughout the world. All these developments, and many others, indicate that culture and cultures will play a much stronger role in the world of the future than they have in the past or do at present.

In the second place, every culture in the world is going through a period of pronounced transformation and change. This is due to many factors, such as the medical, scientific, economic, political, social, demographic, technological, and communications changes going on in the world today, as well as globalization, computerization, digitization, and commercialization. There is scarcely a group of people anywhere in the world that is not wrestling with these changes and with them, the need to determine how they want their cultures to develop in the future.

In the third place, there is the erosion of cultural values, identities, traditions, customs, and ways of life that is occurring in many parts of the world at present—values, identities, traditions, customs, and ways of life that have been built up over decades and often centuries.

In the fourth place, there is much more interaction going on between and among all the different cultures in the world today. While this brings with it many benefits and opportunities—such as learning a great deal more about customs, traditions, and lifestyles that are very different than one's own—it is also increasing the likelihood of cultural conflict and confrontations in the future.

Finally, and most importantly, there is the need for people to play a positive and constructive rather than negative and destructive role in the development of their own culture and the cultures of others. If, as many educators, scholars, and political leaders are predicting, the world is moving into a period of intense cultural interaction, transformation, and change, it only makes sense for people to broaden and deepen their knowledge and understanding of their own culture and the cultures of other countries. While it may never be possible to fully transcend the limits of one's own culture and cultural conditioning, surely the world would be a much better and safer place if people knew and understood a great deal more about their own culture, other cultures in the world, the emerging global culture, and especially the reasons for cultural differences.

Given the need to learn more about culture and cultures, it is imperative to come to grips with the basic changes that are going on in the cultural field today. Fundamental changes are taking place not only in perceptions and definitions of culture but also in the dynamics, characteristics, composition, and functioning of cultures.

Speaking in general terms, there are two main ways of visualizing and defining culture. The first has to do with "the arts, humanities, heritage of history, and finer things in life," and the second has to do with "the whole" or "the total way of life" of people and countries. The first is usually referred to as the traditional or classical way of visualizing and defining culture, whereas the second is usually referred to as the holistic or anthropological way of visualizing and defining culture.[29]

Throughout history, culture has most often been visualized

and defined in terms of the arts, humanities, heritage of history, and finer things in life. This way of perceiving and defining culture is deeply rooted in the practices of most countries and their educational institutions, media outlets, and governments. In recent years, there has been a tendency as indicated earlier to add the "cultural industries" to this list, largely in recognition of the important role these industries now play as "communication channels" or "carriers" of culture.

There are many advantages to visualizing and defining culture the first way. Not only does it highlight many of humanity's most valuable activities and worthwhile pursuits, but it puts the emphasis on things that are concrete, tangible, and specific. Paintings can be seen, films, videos, television programs, and plays can be watched, music can be heard, art galleries and museums can be visited, and books can be read. Presumably this is why most countries, governments, educational institutions, and media outlets prefer to define culture in these terms for funding, administrative, trade, policy, planning, and pedagogical purposes.

During the nineteenth century, however, a second way of perceiving and defining culture emerged to rival the traditional way. It was based on visualizing and defining culture in terms of "the whole" or "the total way of life" of people and countries. This practice commenced when anthropologists and sociologists began studying human collectivities on the ground and in the field in many different parts of the world. They immediately discovered that there were all sorts of words to describe the specific activities that people were engaged in—economic, social, political, agricultural, religious, recreational, artistic, educational, environmental, and so forth. However, there was no word to describe how all these activities were woven together in various combinations and arrangements to form a whole or total way of life.

Culture was the word they used to designate this holistic process and describe this phenomenon. This is why Sir Edward Burnett Tylor, one of the world's first anthropologists, defined culture formally as "that *complex whole* which includes knowledge, belief, art, morals, law, custom, and any other capabilities and habits acquired by [a person] as a member of society."[30] His intention was not to downplay or disregard "the parts of the whole," but rather to recognize and emphasize that the parts are always combined together in different combinations and arrangements to form a whole that is greater than the parts and the sum of the parts.

During the last few decades, there has been a discernible trend throughout the world towards defining culture in these much more expansive terms. After several decades of defining culture using the first, more restrictive definition, UNESCO has stated to define culture in terms of the whole or total way of life of people and countries. This was confirmed at the Second World Conference on Cultural Policies in Mexico City in 1982, as noted in the last chapter.

This trend towards a holistic conception of culture is being driven not only by UNESCO. It is also being espoused by people and countries in all parts of the world. When people and countries are in no danger of losing their culture, it is easy to define culture in the first sense. However, as soon as culture is threatened or there is a real danger of losing it, it is amazing how quickly there is a sudden realization of its holistic character. Clearly there is nothing quite like the threat of cultural extinction or foreign domination to bring about a rapid realization of the holistic nature and all-encompassing character of culture.

When culture is defined in this way, it is concerned with all groups, classes, activities, institutions, and people and not just some of them. Culture is all-inclusive in this sense. It is education as well as economics; the sciences as well as the arts; recreation as well as religion; sports and social affairs as well as technology and communications; popular music as well as classical music; politics as well as industry, and on and on it goes.

This is what more and more people in the world mean today when they say they are "products of their culture." They are saying that they are the products of everything that exists in their culture, or their culture *as a whole*. Presumably this is why Wole Soyinka, the African Nobel laureate, views culture as "*source*"—the source from which all things flow and to which all things return.[31] It is a way of thinking about and visualizing culture that has much more to do with culture as "the whole" than it does with culture as "a part or parts of the whole."

When culture is visualized in these terms, it is concerned with the entire way people "visualize and interpret the world, organize themselves, conduct their affairs, elevate and embellish life, act in the world, and position themselves in the world."[32] This shines the spotlight squarely on the worldviews, values, and value systems that people use to bind all the component parts of their culture together to form a whole or total way of life, and consequently on such key relationships as the relationship between people and the natural environment, consumption and conservation, materialism and spiritualism, affluence and poverty, the quantitative and qualitative dimensions of life, and many more.

Thus it becomes clear why a shift is occurring in the world from the traditional way of viewing culture to the holistic way.

Without a much better understanding of the worldviews, values, and value systems that people use to bind the component parts of their cultures together to form an organic and integrated whole, it may not be possible to come to grips with the host of difficult, demanding, and dangerous problems confronting the world. This makes broadening and deepening knowledge and understanding of the holistic character of culture a categorical imperative.

So is learning about cultures. If fundamental changes are going on in how culture is perceived and defined, fundamental changes are also going on in the way cultures are perceived and defined, especially in terms of their composition, character, characteristics, and functioning.

During the nineteenth and early twentieth century, it was customary to view cultures largely in uniform, homogeneous, and closed terms. The focus was on developing cultures that were internally inclusive, externally delineated, concerned with similarities much more than differences, and preoccupied largely with creating a national identity, soul, and spirit. While this led to the creation of many valuable artistic, scholarly, literary, and philosophical works, it also contributed to intensive and excessive nationalism, the fighting of two world wars, the slaughter of millions of people, and the clash of different cultures and civilizations.

International events over the last fifty years have served to alter this situation, although there are still many exceptions to the general rule. For one thing, it is now generally recognized that there are very real dangers when cultures are uniform, homogeneous and closed. Mircea Malitza, the Romanian scholar and statesman, summed this problem up most effectively when he said:

> Cultures in watertight compartments are doomed to oblivion. Dialogue is essential. The choice between the development of a national culture and an increase in exchanges with the outside world is a false one. Interdependence cannot be denied. The cultures which have blossomed are those which have had the advantage of innumerable influences, received and transmitted in accordance with a process of unceasing enrichment.[33]

As a result of realizations like this, and many others, cultures are becoming much more diverse, open, and heterogeneous today. Developments in transportation, trade, communications, technology, politics, finance, and globalization are making it impossible to shut out influences from other parts of the world. Moreover, there is much more cultural interaction and exchange going on today, not only between cultures, but also within them. While this has been slowed by the COVID-19 pandemic, there is still a great deal of interracial, ethnic, and cultural mixing going on as a result of demographic developments and tourist activities, migratory movements, interracial marriages, texting and mass media linkages, and transformations in social structures and institutions. As a result of these developments, and others, most cultures are becoming more pluralistic, multiracial, and diverse, with many different ethnic, racial, religious, and linguistic groups, subcultures, and social, economic, political and technological activities interacting under one roof. This brings with it a new set of cultural requirements and problems, especially as more conflicts now take place within countries than between countries.

This necessitates *new* understandings of the challenges facing cultures. Whereas the challenge in earlier times was to achieve "unity in similarity" through a homogeneous way of life and uniform national identity, the challenge today is to achieve "unity in diversity" through heterogeneous ways of life and multiple identities. This will require the development of many more links and connections between and within all the diverse subcultures, racial groups, ethnic and religious communities, and different activities that comprise cultures. Coexistence, cross-fertilization, dialogue, exchange, and cooperation—rather than isolation, separation, delineation, and competition—are now the order of the day.

If profound changes are going on in the composition, dynamics, and characteristics of cultures, profound changes are also going on in the international character of cultures. It would not be far off the mark to say that virtually all cultures in the world today—including the smallest, most remote, most inconspicuous, and marginalized—are becoming "world cultures" in the sense that they are compelled to deal with all the changes going on in the world and are unable to tune out developments taking place elsewhere. While in previous decades and centuries it was possible for cultures to remain isolated, today this is no longer possible.

Viewed from this perspective, one of the biggest challenges confronting people and countries in all parts of the world today will be to maintain adequate control over the decision-making processes affecting their cultures and ways of life while simultaneously learning to function effectively in a global world. People know their cultures must change. What they are opposed to—and opposed to in increasing numbers—is not change, but rather developments that serve the interests of corporate and affluent elites rather than themselves. This is why people everywhere in the world are demanding the right to decide for themselves how their cultures will change, as well as how they will order the component parts of their cultures and cultural life to form a cohesive and coherent entity.

Given all the changes going on with respect to culture and cultures in the world today, there is an urgent need for people to learn much more about culture and cultures in the broader, deeper, and more fundamental holistic sense. This is an exceedingly difficult task since few educational institutions provide opportunities to do this at present. This means that if people want to learn more about culture and cultures in this sense, they will have to do so largely through self-discovery, self-instruction, lifelong learning, adult education and extension courses, and personal observations and experiences, until educational institutions catch up and make the changes that are required to incorporate this type of learning into their programs.

It is one thing to learn about culture and cultures when they are visualized and dealt with in terms of the arts, humanities, heritage of history, cultural industries, and finer things in life. Here, knowledge and understanding come from products and activities that can be seen, touched, talked about, traded, transported, and enjoyed. However, when culture and cultures are thought about in holistic terms they cannot be understood in this concrete, material, and specific sense. They are far too complex, vast, and multidimensional to do so. Moreover, as noted earlier, it is not possible to *see* culture and cultures as wholes or to see the organizational principles and practices that are used to create them. Nor it is possible to *know* all the myriad activities, institutions, worldviews, values, value systems, and parts that comprise them. This means that people must learn to *sense* and *feel* how culture and cultures are structured and put together as wholes, as well as to piece together general impressions and visualizations of culture and cultures from a variety of sources, experiences, perspectives, and possibilities.

For Giles Gunn, an internationally recognized cultural scholar, the best place to start to get to know culture and cultures as wholes—and indeed any type of human whole—is through the parts and the dynamic interplay that is constantly going on between and among the parts and the whole:

> We cannot understand the parts of anything without some sense of the whole to which they belong, just as we cannot comprehend the whole to which they belong until we have grasped the parts that make it up. Thus we are constantly obliged to move back and forth in our effort to understand something "between the whole conceived through the parts which actualize it and the parts conceived through the whole which motivates them" in an effort "to turn them, by a sort of intellectual perpetual motion, into explication of one another."[34]

It follows from this that if people want to learn more about culture and cultures in general and their own culture in particular in the comprehensive and all-inclusive sense, they should start with their own specific part of the whole. This could be their job, life, or geographical location in the world. However, it is not their job, life, or geographical location considered in isolation, but rather as part of the larger fabric of their culture as a whole. In other words, it is the details of their own specific circumstances and experiences considered in terms of the larger cultural context within which these circumstances and experiences are situated.

To progress further in this area, it is necessary to focus attention on things and institutions that function as wholes, and therefore have a great deal to tell us about how culture and cultures function in the holistic sense. The most obvious examples of this are people's families, neighbourhoods, communities, towns, cities, and regions.

Every family is a whole composed of many interconnected parts. This is apparent as soon as family members transcend their own specific experiences and become aware of the family as a holistic entity. When this happens, it is apparent that families are constantly evolving and changing in the comprehensive sense, as changes take place in the lives of individual family members and especially in the relationships between and among family members. The similarities to cultures here are striking, since cultures are also constantly evolving and changing as dynamic changes take place in the component parts that constitute them.

Nor is this all. Families also provide countless other ways to learn about culture and cultures. Not only is every family member distinct, different, and unique—thereby providing valuable learning opportunities for all family members—but every family is also deeply rooted in a specific culture or several different cultures. This brings with it a wealth of possibilities. It is amazing how much people can learn about their own culture and the cultures of others by exploring the genealogical roots and historical traditions of their family members. This is especially true when past and present family members come from a variety of ethnic backgrounds and cultural origins, or when they have been involved in a single culture over a long period of time.

What is true of families is also true of neighbourhoods, communities, towns, cities, and regions. These complex entities are also wholes composed of many interrelated parts. As such, they provide ideal learning opportunities and models for people interested in broadening and deepening their understanding of how culture and cultures are put together and function.

Like families, neighbourhoods, communities, towns, cities, and regions also possess all sorts of fascinating treasures located just beneath the surface. Furthermore, they are close at hand. And yet, how often do we take the time and trouble to dig deeply into these human collectivities to acquaint ourselves with the fascinating array of programs, activities, resources, and experiences that are available to enrich our understanding of them, and therefore our own culture and possibly other cultures in the world? A little curiosity here can bring numerous rewards by opening up a vast panorama of possibilities, including exposing the numerous layers and levels of a culture, its diverse ethnic and racial groups, countless multicultural events and activities, unique customs and traditions, and scintillating sights, sounds, smells, textures, and tastes. These help to broaden and deepen our knowledge and understanding of neighbourhoods, communities, towns, cities, and regions, and with them, culture and cultures.

It is through intensive examination of these possibilities that it is possible to slowly but surely piece together images or impressions of the distinctive character and ambiance of the aforementioned entities as organic and dynamic wholes. Amos Rapoport explains this process in terms of cities:

> In dealing with the urban order, it may be useful to begin with the sensory, experiential qualities of cities which are also organized and ordered. Cities, among other things, are physical artifacts, experienced through all the

> senses by people who are in them. They are experienced sequentially as people follow different paths and use different movement modes through them. Cities look, smell, sound and *feel* different; they have a different character or *ambience*. This is easily felt, but it is very difficult to describe.[35]

Familiarity with the distinctive character and ambience of various places provides a valuable step towards what Raymond Williams, the cultural scholar and historian, calls "*the structure of feeling*" of cultures. While this structure of feeling is less specific than more traditional notions of national identity and national cultural character—but also less prone to nationalism, chauvinism, and racism—it represents the bundle of beliefs, convictions, axioms, myths, and assumptions used to bind cultures together and determine people's actions, attitudes, preferences and behavioural characteristics in them:

> More overt and explicit than some underlying collective unconscious but less determinate and intellectualizable than an ideology, a structure of feeling is the "particular and characteristic colour" that the ensemble of the values, beliefs, and practices of a given culture imparts to the experiences of its members. In particular, a given culture's structure of feeling will at least influence if not determine the patterns of response of its members in resolving or coping with the dilemmas and contradictions that confront them in their daily lives. For Williams, the principal aim of cultural analysis is to discern and understand this structure of feeling as it manifests itself throughout the entire range of a given culture's expressions.[36]

For people interested in learning about "the structure of feeling" of their own culture and the cultures of others—and therefore the worldviews, values, value systems, codes, recipes, and ordering processes that people use to create the structure of feeling of their cultures as wholes—it is helpful to turn to artists, scholars, architects, critics, and other creative people. These are the people who possess the intuitive and sensorial skills as well as the expressive, imaginative, and communicative abilities that are needed to "sense" how cultures are put together as structures of feeling and as dynamic and organic wholes made up of countless parts, and who communicate this to others. They are able to do so through their ability to create signs, myths, legends, metaphors, stories, similes, and especially symbols that "stand for the whole" and convey a vast amount of information about the whole, as we discussed in the chapter on arts education. Think of the symbolic importance of artistic works by Rabindranath Tagore and Ravi Shankar for Indian culture, Gabriel Garcia Márquez for Columbian culture, Gabriela Mistral for Chilean culture, and Astor Piazzolla and Jorge Luis Borges for Argentinian culture as ideal examples of this. If, as Gandhi maintained, "a nation's culture resides in the hearts and the soul of its people," then without doubt the arts are the gateway to cultures in this sense.

While artists, scholars, architects, critics, and other types of creative people are excellent vehicles for helping people to visualize, sense, feel, and understand cultures as wholes through the symbolic works they create, they are not the only means of doing this. The cultural industries also do so, because they provide the communication channels and distributive mechanisms, devices, and networks that are needed to make the works of artists, architects, scholars, critics, and other types of artistic people known to the general public. Athletes and sports organizations play an important role as well because they represent parts of cultural wholes that transmit strong messages and signals about the structure and characteristics of their cultures through sports. Anthropological, sociological, and cultural interpretations of history are also important because they tend to deal with the totality of cultures, and therefore the patterns, value systems, social structures, interrelationships, and worldviews that constitute cultures. Personality studies help us understand culture in the all-inclusive sense because, as Ruth Benedict contended, cultures are really "personalities writ large." Philosophical studies and theological treatises also have much to say, because they deal with human conduct in a variety of spiritual, religious, and cultural settings. And ecological, economic, geographical, and historical studies reveal how cultures imprint their ways of life and structures of feeling on very distinct parts of the world's geography as well as the natural, historical, and global environment.

What is steadily unfolding here are some of the most important ways people can broaden and deepen their knowledge and understanding of culture and cultures in general and their own culture and cultures in particular. When this is combined with other learning opportunities—visits to libraries, use of computer facilities and internet sites, formation of workshops and study groups, lifelong learning programs, adult education and extension courses, foreign language studies, visits to ethnic cultural centres, travels to other countries to experience other people's cultures first hand, and so forth—a broad spectrum of options and opportunities emerge that help people to learn much more about culture and cultures outside the formal educational system.

Many of the "new learning communities" that are springing up around the world have an important role to play in this regard. Awareness of this role emanates from the fact that there is an intimate connection between culture, cultures, and the learning process, since culture and cultures impact on the learning process and the learning process impacts on culture and cultures.

This is evident in a variety of ways. When culture and cultures are understood in holistic terms, they provide the context or "container" within which all education and learning takes place. As such, they influence what people learn, how they learn, and why they learn. This process is often called "enculturation," since it describes the process whereby people are prepared for participation and citizenship in the specific cultures in which they are living and working. This takes place through exposure to—and education in—the worldviews, values, value systems, and lifestyles that are most characteristic of these cultures and form the basis of cultural life.

New learning communities can play a valuable role in this by helping people to see more clearly the strengths and shortcomings of their own culture as well as their cultural conditioning and enculturation process. This serves a useful purpose because it helps people discover what needs to be learned about their culture to function effectively in it and live a cultural life, as well as to assess their culture in objective and impartial terms to see where it comes up short. The most obvious example of this is the impact that all people's cultures are having on the natural environment and the dire need to change this.

Since many of the new learning communities exist outside the formal educational system, they are also in a better position to help people assess the worldviews, values, and value systems of their cultures, thereby helping them to ascertain what is appropriate and what is inappropriate in their culture. Worldviews, values, and value systems based on exerting or imposing control over nature, promoting excessive consumption and production, accepting inequalities in the distribution of income, wealth, resources, and power, fostering and promoting social and economic inequalities, and treating people unfairly should be contested regardless of one's own cultural conditioning and enculturation process. Goethe provided wise advice in this regard when he said, "Your own epoch you cannot change. You can, however, oppose its trends and lay the groundwork for auspicious developments."[37]

Ultimately, there is no substitute for providing comprehensive cultural education in all educational institutions and systems throughout the world. This education should start early in life and end late, as well as be incorporated fully into children's early development, extended through their elementary, secondary, and post-secondary education, sustained later in life through adult education and extension courses, and, equally essential, maintained during the final stages of life.

Unfortunately, few educational institutions in the world are equipped to provide the kind of comprehensive cultural education that is required at this time. This is due to the lack of qualitied and well-trained teachers in this field, as well as the fact that very few teaching and learning materials are available that discuss culture in general and cultures in particular as complex wholes and total ways of life. While some schools provide "multicultural days" that are designed to introduce students to different cultures in the world through their food, foodstuffs, cuisines, dances, customs, and traditions—and others celebrate specific ethnic holidays and events for similar purposes—these activities are usually extracurricular rather than curricular in nature and therefore fall far short of the fully developed, lifelong cultural education that is necessary.

To be effective, cultural education should encompass four distinct components. The first component is learning about the "*nature and meaning of culture in general and cultures in particular in all their diverse forms and manifestations.*" This is necessary because there is a great deal of misunderstanding, confusion, and controversy throughout the world today over the nature and meaning of culture and cultures that needs to be clarified and rectified through exposure to all the principal manifestations of culture and cultures that exist in the world. In order for this type of education to be effective, it should reveal that perceiving and defining culture in terms of the arts, humanities, heritage of history, finer things in life, and the cultural industries—which is still commonplace in most educational institutions, corporations, foundations, and governments today—is only one of a number of basic definitions of culture and cultures that exist. Others, including anthropological, sociological, ecological, biological, and cosmological manifestations of culture, are gaining greater acceptance because they are more relevant to the problems confronting humanity at present and the need to find successful solutions to these problems in the future.

The second component should focus on "*the fundamentals of culture and cultures.*" This is essential because all cultures are predicated on certain underlying axioms, worldviews, values, values systems, principles, beliefs, and ideals that shed light on how these cultures are structured as dynamic and organic wholes as well as on how they function in the world in both theoretical and practical terms.

The third component should concentrate on studying "*the contents and parts of culture and cultures.*" This should include all the different activities that make up culture and cultures, how some of these activities act as symbols and gateways to broader and deeper understandings of culture and cultures through this symbolic process, and especially what cultural scholars have had to say about the importance of these matters. This is a crucial component in cultural education because it is impossible to see or know culture and cultures in the holistic sense without selecting the parts that are the most representative. It doesn't take a great deal of imagination to think of how pictures, portraits, images, and visualizations of all the different cultures in the world can be created though this miraculous symbolic and all-encompassing process.

The final component of a comprehensive cultural education should deal with the "*context of cultures.*" This involves studying how culture and cultures are situated in the natural, historical, and global environment—in other words, in space and time—as well as how they are affected by a host of factors and activities such as economics, politics, technology, the world system, worldviews, values, and beliefs. This is one of the most critical elements in cultural education of all because "context determines contents," as Ruth Benedict consistently contended.

Initially, cultural education should focus on the cultures of the countries people are living in. However, eventually it should fan out and be complemented and enriched by courses that juxtapose, compare, and contrast the different cultures of the world: African, Asian, North American, European, Middle Eastern, and South American; western and eastern; northern and southern; indigenous, imposed, and imported; homogeneous and heterogeneous; popular and elite; and so forth. There is a vast spectrum of knowledge, information, ideas, and ideals in these cultures that needs to be pulled together and presented in one place, as well as classified in different ways and made available to people on a regular, sustained, and systematic basis.

Just as it is possible to learn a great deal about all the religions in the world from courses in comparative religions, so it is possible to learn an enormous amount about all the cultures in the world through courses in comparative cultures. If, as the old saying states, "all is known by comparison," then comparisons between cultures are very valuable because they reveal an incredible amount about the similarities and differences that exist between and among all the diverse cultures of the world—similarities and differences that are due to significant differences in those cultures' origins, historical development, customs, traditions, traits, behavioural characteristics, functioning, and overall ways of life.

All this will broaden, deepen, and enrich people's lives in numerous ways. Studying the rich cornucopia of cultures that exists throughout the world will make it possible to cultivate more effective ways of seeing, acting, behaving, believing, valuing, and living in the world; to accept and appreciate other people, customs, traditions, cultures, and civilizations; to expand consciousness and mindfulness, enhance welfare and well-being, and improve individual and collective well-being, behavior, and lifestyles; to increase employment opportunities; to learn other languages; and, in sum, to experience a great deal more happiness, fulfillment, and creativity in life. Without a much better understanding of all the diverse cultures in the world, it is difficult to see how the world can ever become a more secure, harmonious, and peaceful place for all people, cultures, and countries.

Chapter 10

Feasting on Cultures to Solve Our Problems and Enhance Our Lives

I do not want my house to be walled in on all sides and my windows to be stuffed. I want the culture of all the lands to be blown about my house as freely as possible. But I refuse to be blown off my feet by any.

—Mahatma Gandhi[38]

I have had the good fortune to be born in Toronto and spend the bulk of my life there. I say "good fortune" because I have been drawing on all the diverse cultures of this remarkable city to enhance my life for more than three-quarters of a century.

When I went to elementary school, I discovered that most of the kids at the school I attended were also born in Toronto and had European roots like myself. Some had Scottish, Irish, English, or German roots. Others had Italian, Greek, or Ukrainian roots. And a few had Czechoslovakian, Yugoslavian, Romanian, or Jewish roots. We quickly learned not to talk about our ethnic origins because this caused tensions that interfered with our natural desire to play together and have a good time together.

Being born to parents who had European roots had its advantages. Consistent with the values and traditions of most European countries and their cultures, my parents were anxious to see that I got a solid grounding and excellent education in the arts. So they sent me to the Art Gallery of Toronto for art lessons, paid for private piano and singing lessons, and enrolled me in a church choir at Grace Church on-the-Hill, as mentioned earlier. While I didn't realize it at the time, I was drawing on other cultures and their well-established commitment to the arts to broaden my horizons and enhance my education and life.

When I went to secondary school, most of the students I associated and hung around with were Jewish. This was because there were many more Jewish students at the secondary school I attended than at elementary school and they seemed to be interested in many of the same things that were of interest to me. It was a good thing they were Jewish because they dragged me along to university with them as a result of their keen desire for education. Had it not been for this, I probably would not have gone to university because academically I did very badly at secondary school. Here again, I was drawing on another culture—in this case Jewish culture and its well-known reverence for education and learning—to enhance my situation and bring about a fundamental change in my life. It is a change that made it possible for me to reap numerous rewards.

There were many other rewards to be reaped from my association with Jewish students at secondary school. One was going to the YMHA—the Young Men's Hebrew Association—at the corner of Bloor Street and Spadina Avenue to play basketball. Another was playing billiards on Brunswick Avenue. And a third was going out to eat after our basketball games at the Mars Restaurant on College Street, the Crescent Grill on Spadina Avenue, and other restaurants in the central part of Toronto.

It was also through my friends at the "Y" that I got my first taste of Chinese food. While my father had taken us to Studleighs for many years—a Victorian restaurant on King Street that was famous for its roast beef, buffets, and mile-high mincemeat pies—this was the extent of my exposure to food from other cultures until my friends at the "Y" took me to 12A, a small Chinese restaurant above a store on Elizabeth Street in the area of Toronto known as Chinatown.

I will never forget my first Chinese meal. It consisted of won ton soup, barbecued pork spare ribs, shrimp fried rice, beef chow mien, sweet and sour chicken balls, and fortune cookies. I remember thinking, "What have I been missing all these years!" Anyone who has grown up on food from Great Britain will know exactly what I mean, since most of our meals consisted of meat, potatoes, and a vegetable. My mouth still waters when I think about my first Chinese meal. I can taste it today like it was just yesterday.

Chinese food has been an integral part of my life ever since. For years, I went to the Sai Woo restaurant on Dundas near Bay. It was extremely popular with many Torontonians because its founder—Bill Wen—knew how to throw a banquet and was renowned in Toronto for helping Chinese immigrants and participating in the creation of a home for the aged in the downtown area. Like many residents of Toronto, I can still recall his superb banquets with their scrumptious dishes, impeccable service, excellent organization, centuries-old decorative eggs, and other colourful decorations. It is probably the closest I will ever come to knowing what it was like to eat at the court of Kublai Khan and other Chinese rulers.

Like residents and visitors alike, I have been enjoying the cuisines of the many different cultures that exist in Toronto ever since I had my first Chinese meal. Unlike Chinese cuisine, which has been available in Toronto for a long time, most of the cuisines of other cultures are more recent arrivals. For example, I was one of the first residents in this city to experience Indian food and "hot cuisine" when the Rajput restaurant opened its doors on Bloor near Bathurst in the 1960s, with its pungent curries, biryanis, pakoras, and other delicacies.

And while we are on Bloor Street, what about the Country Style restaurant? It opened its doors after the Hungarian Revolution in 1956 and served some of the best home-cooked Hungarian dishes I have ever tasted, which is saying a great deal because my parents took in a Hungarian refugee after the revolution and he cooked many marvellous Hungarian meals for us. However, he couldn't match the Country Style for its cauliflower soup, humongous wiener schnitzels, chicken paprikash, lecsó, cherry strudel, and its quaint cooks in high-laced boots.

For many years, several Italian restaurants on St. Clair Avenue near Dufferin and on College Street near Euclid Avenue were favourites, as was the Balkans restaurant on Elm Street. In fact, this wonderful restaurant—with its stoic owner in a maroon fez and tassel—was my favourite restaurant in Toronto. It specialized in Yugoslavian cuisine, and its "Balkan dinner" of Serbian bean soup, breaded mushrooms with a fantastic tartar sauce, ćevapčići, raznjici, and backlava was "to die for," as they say. It was the perfect introduction to the entire Balkans region that I visited many times in the years to follow to enjoy its rich cultures and traditions. I regret the day the Balkans restaurant closed in Toronto more than any other change that has taken place in this city since that time. It moved to Mount Pleasant Avenue in uptown Toronto for a time after it left its location on Elm Street in downtown Toronto. Unfortunately, it was not the same. Things seldom are.

The list certainly does not end here. For many years, I enjoyed a Turkish restaurant on Dundas Street West and a Japanese restaurant in Don Mills that never failed to excite. And more recently, I have enjoyed Thai cuisine in the many Thai restaurants that have opened up in Toronto in recent years. I remember thinking when I had my first taste of Thai food in Bangkok on my way to New Zealand to conduct a UNESCO mission that it was too bad Torontonians did not know a great deal more about Thai cuisine, which is one of the finest cuisines in the world. It seemed to incorporate the best of Indian and Chinese cooking, with a bit of tropical excitement and a great deal of artistry thrown in for good measure. So it is not without a certain sense of satisfaction that I witness the current love affair between Torontonians and Thai cuisine.

I could go on and on, but the point has been made. Our lives are incredibly enhanced and enriched by our ability to tap into other cultures through their cuisines. While this is only one small aspect of cultures, it is a very important aspect because most of us are first exposed to other cultures through their cuisines.

Whether Brazilian, Belgian, Indonesian, or any other culture, the cuisines of the various cultures of the world bring joy into our lives like nothing else. I know people who no longer ask if you would like to eat fish, chicken, or steak for dinner, but rather whether you would like to eat "Indian," Moroccan," "French," "Italian," "South American," "Caribbean," or "Chinese."

Thelma Barer-Stein knows all about this. In her fascinating book, *You Eat What You Are: A Study of Ethnic Food Traditions*, she states, "Without food we cannot survive. But food is much more than a tool of survival. Food is a source of pleasure, comfort, security. Food is also a symbol of hospitality, social status, and has ritual significance. What we select to eat, how we prepare it, serve it, and even how we eat it, are all factors deeply touched by our individual [and collective!] cultural inheritance."[39]

One organization that has been instrumental in expanding and promoting the importance of agricultural diversity, culture, creativity, craftsmanship, and cuisine, as well as many other activities closely connected to this, is the International Institute of Gastronomy, Culture, Arts and Tourism (IGCAT), located in Spain. Co-founded and spearheaded by Diane Dodd and her colleagues, this remarkable organization has done a great deal since its inception just a decade ago to celebrate cultural and food diversity, largely by recognizing and providing awards to outstanding regions that connect different sectors in an endeavour to promote a sustainable future and show how the gastronomic and culinary arts are intimately connected to people's overall health and well-being, other artistic and cultural activities, responsible tourism, environmental conservation, and sustainable development. In so doing, they are making a strong case for the fact that food, foodstuffs, and the gastronomic and culinary arts, like all other art forms, are "gateways" to culture and cultures, with much to learn from them.

Take China and Chinese culture as an obvious example. Regardless of how many dynasties have existed in China, Chinese culture as a whole is based on the principle of yin and yang or the theory of opposites: male and female, light and dark, positive and negative, and so forth. Success in life comes from how well people deal with these opposites and achieve balance, harmony, and synergy. It is not surprising, therefore, that Chinese cuisine is also based on opposites—sweet and sour, hot and cold, spicy and mild, and so forth—as well as how well these opposites are blended together to form a harmonious whole.

Japanese culture provides another interesting illustration of this. It is a well-known fact that Japanese culture is concerned with "simplicity." The objective is to make things as simple as possible with the least amount of aggravation and complication. Japanese cuisine also embodies this objective, since the challenge is to create superb gastronomic experiences with the least amount of complexity and confusion. Hence the emphasis on dishes and meals that are aesthetically pleasing, exquisitely served, delicious to eat, sophisticated, yet very simple.

Of course, the culinary arts are not the only arts that act as a gateway to cultures. The crafts do this, too, and do it very well. Like different cuisines, the crafts enhance our lives, which is why most people are anxious to decorate their homes with craft objects from different cultures.

I discovered this many years ago when I was scouring Toronto looking for craft objects to beautify our home. I quickly learned that there are many areas of Toronto where exquisite craft objects from the world's different cultures can be found. Roncesvalles Avenue, for example, was perfect for Polish crafts, particularly table runners and hand-carved wooden plates with scenes from the Tatras Mountains on them. Bloor Street West, in an area known as "The Village," was ideal for Ukrainian crafts, especially pots, bowls, and tablecloths with incredible geometric shapes and colourful designs on them. College Street, between Bathurst and Spadina, was unbeatable for South American and Spanish crafts—everything from superb leatherwork and replicas of El Cid, Don Quixote, and Sancho Panza to painted plates like the ones that once graced the walls of Carman's steakhouse on Alexander Street. And speaking of painted plates, are there any that are more beautiful than the ones created in Turkey? They can occasionally be found in craft stores in Toronto if one is very lucky, with their incredible designs of flowers, plants, and trees on them.

And while it came a little later when people from Iran and

other parts of the Middle East started showing up in Toronto in large numbers, what about carpets? Is there anything more beautiful to warm a room or enhance a wall than a carpet from Iran, Turkestan, or some other Middle Eastern country? The very names of the cities that have made these carpets world famous—Tabriz, Qum, Kashan, Bakhitiari, Shiraz, Kirman, Meshed, Bokhara, and the like—conjure up images of the *Arabian Nights*, religious motifs, and mythological themes. Does anything say more about the cultures of these countries and parts of the world than their carpets?

Not long after I started scouring the city looking for craft objects, I became aware of Toronto's greatest resource. I am speaking, of course, of its ethnic neighbourhoods. Has anything done more to bring vitality, variety, colour, and character to this city?

At a time when Jane Jacobs was making the case that neighbourhoods play a crucial role in the lives of all people and cities, I was exploring Toronto's many distinct ethnic neighbourhoods to see what I could find. These neighbourhoods held a particular fascination for me because I could visit any part of the world without ever having to leave Toronto.

Whenever I felt the need to "get away" or "take a trip abroad"—which was frequently the case when I was working at the Ontario Arts Council and teaching at York University and the University of Toronto—I would take off for "Little Italy," "Little Portugal," "Little India," "Little Greece," "Chinatown," or some other fascinating destination. I would spend a full day there feeling like I was in a totally different part of the world: shopping in different shops; talking to people who had very different ethnic origins and cultural backgrounds than I did; and eating meals that were simply out of this world. I would then return to my own culture and part of the world feeling relaxed, revitalized, and refreshed. And the best part of all was that I didn't have to pay an arm and a leg to get there, be at the airport three hours before departure, battle with baggage clerks, and endure countless other inconveniences.

Of all my explorations in Toronto, my favourite one was walking the entire length of Bloor Street and Danforth Avenue. Here is what I would do. I would drive my car to the Warden Avenue subway station, park it, and then take the train to the Royal York subway station at the other end of the line. I would then walk back along Bloor Street to the Bloor Viaduct, and then along Danforth Avenue (the continuation of Bloor Street on the eastern side of the Don Valley) to the Warden Avenue subway station. It would take a whole day to complete this journey, but was it ever worth it! What an incredible eye opener it was. Talk about tapping into other cultures to solve our problems and enhance our lives! I learned so much about life and living by walking and talking my way through a vast variety of cultures—Ukrainian, Polish, Indian, Italian, Somalian, Caribbean, Korean, British, Greek, Macedonian, and so forth. Anyone who has walked this route will know exactly what I mean. It was even possible to experience a bit of "The Rock"—the culture of Newfoundland—at Danforth and Broadview before entering Greektown and enjoying Greek culture between Chester and Pape.

And while we are talking about enjoying a variety of different cultural experiences, what about Caravan for a cultural experience *par excellence*? While there are now many other ways to experience the different cultures of the world in Toronto than when Caravan first began its operations in the 1970s, who is not exceedingly grateful to Zena and Leon Kossar—

two Ukrainian Canadians—for creating this magnificent opportunity to experience a "smorgasbord of cultures" through their arts, crafts, people, and cuisines? For a small price, it was possible to purchase a passport that entitled the bearer to visit an array of ethnic pavilions located in different parts of the city. They had everything: song, dance, drink, drama, poetry, music, storytelling, food, craft objects, and people in their native costumes from virtually every culture and country in the world. A veritable feast and a real pioneer in confirming and exposing Toronto's multicultural roots and multiracial character.

While opportunities like this abound in Toronto today since the city is deemed one of the most cosmopolitan in the world, most people do not venture too far beyond this. While they may feel comfortable eating other people's food, enjoying their songs, dances, craft objects, and community celebrations, exploring their shops, and walking in their neighbourhoods, they feel uncomfortable digging deeper into their cultures. While there are many reasons for this—such as not knowing the language of the culture they are experiencing, or feeling that they are intruding—this is most unfortunate. For what they will discover if they take the time and trouble and demonstrate a bit of courage, imagination, trust, and initiative is that there are countless possibilities to address their problems and enhance their lives through interactions with the different cultures of the world.

I discovered this many years ago when I was experiencing some difficulties with my own culture and its preoccupation with materialism, money, and commercialism. Although I had grown up in a culture that was predominantly English-speaking and heavily oriented towards Great Britain and the United States, I was doing some work for Canada's Department of

External Affairs at the time that brought me into contact with many French-speaking people closely associated with French and Quebec culture. I quickly learned that French-speaking people have a very different "take" on life and living. While they are not averse to materialism, money, and commercialism, they are much more concerned with *joie de vivre*, and how to get the most out of life. Had it not been for this, I doubt very much that I would have found the insights that were needed to live a full, well-rounded, and balanced life—a life that has brought me an enormous amount of pleasure and satisfaction over the years.

Many years later, I had a very different experience with another culture, but one that improved and enhanced my life in equal measure. Here is how it came about.

I had long thought of taking art lessons to provide some relief from being an author, as well as creating a hobby I could enjoy later in life. But I had always abandoned these thoughts as quickly as they entered my mind because I didn't have the money that was needed to purchase a drafting table and all the other equipment and supplies that were necessary for this.

One day, I was walking in our neighbourhood and happened to see a huge drafting table on a front lawn with a sign on it saying, "I'm yours for free if you can promise me a good home and look after me properly." I immediately thought, "This is the answer to my prayers!" I dashed to the house of a friend who had a large panel truck and asked him if he would help me move the drafting table into our basement. As luck would have it, I was walking in the Market Village Mall in Markham on the outskirts of Toronto a few days later and I happened to see another sign saying, "Brush painting classes given here." I instantly signed up for these classes, which were given by Mr. Lawrence Lui and the Federation of Chinese Canadians of Markham.

It wasn't long before I was learning a great deal about brush painting, including how to hold and load the brush, mix the colours and paints, and create landscapes. I also learned a great deal about many other aspects of Chinese culture, including why brush painting is such a revered art form in China—an art form intimately connected with nature and possessing a tradition stretching back over a thousand years. Small wonder the Chinese have a special affinity for birds, fish, horses, trees, flowers, mountains, water, rivers, the lotus, and the bamboo, since these things figure prominently in Chinese brush paintings and many other aspects of Chinese culture.

I also learned a great deal about some of the most important natural and human-made wonders in China and Chinese culture, such as Suzhou, the garden city, Xian, the ancient capital, Hangzhou, the city of lakes, Guilin, the Venice of the Far East, and the world famous Huangshan Mountains. But more important than anything else, I learned why calligraphy is deemed to be one of the greatest art forms and cultural resources in China. Just as it is impossible to understand Persian culture without understanding the crucial role that carpets play in it, so it is impossible to understand Chinese culture without understanding the quintessential role of calligraphy in it.

More recently, I have been delving into other aspects of Chinese culture. I was experiencing some health problems at one time and wondered if there was anything in Chinese culture that might help me to deal with these problems. I had long been aware that oriental cultures place a high priority on achieving and maintaining good health—the practice of yoga, for example—and have always been intrigued by the number of Chinese people doing Tai Chi, Qi Gong, and other forms of physical, recreational, and spiritual activity in the parks in and around Toronto. I had a chance to get involved in these activities first hand one winter's day when I decided to take up walking at the Markville Mall. It wasn't long before I discovered that there was a group of people at the Mall, mostly women, doing "Lee's Taiji" and "Yuanji Dance." Basically, this is a health system that incorporates various aspects of Tai Chi, Qi Gong, and other Chinese health, exercise, and movement systems. For about an hour every morning, the group was doing a variety of exercises set to the most exquisite music imaginable. This was followed by several minutes of massaging the different parts of the body, especially hands, face, arms, legs, knees, nose, head, stomach, kidneys, and lower back.

One morning I was watching this group going through its daily exercises when one of the members of the class asked me to join in. I think she sensed I was intrigued by what I saw and was "ripe for the picking," as they say. So this is what I did. I joined the group and have now been doing Tai Chi and Qi Gong exercises for about thirteen years, first with this group and more recently with a wonderful group called Hong Kei. What an invigorating experience this has been! I am feeling better—standing straighter, breathing deeper, relaxing more, and walking tall—and am learning a great deal about my body, its various dantian centres, acupuncture points, and the storage, retrieval and movement of *chi*—energy—in my body. The people in this group are so helpful, cheerful, and full of life that I enjoy my experiences with them immensely. I am feeling infused with their energy, vitality, and love of life, and am even learning a few words of Cantonese, Mandarin, and Hakka in the process.

And this is the point. There are countless ways to solve our problems and enhance our lives through involvement in other cultures and the numerous insights, assets, and capabilities they have built up over the centuries. Whether it is through the arts, crafts, cuisine, healthcare, literature, religion, languages, or entire ways of life, the diverse cultures of the world are capable of producing enormous benefits for us in ways we can scarcely imagine. And there are always people in these cultures—warm, sensitive, compassionate, and caring people—who are "there for us" and anxious to welcome us into their cultures and assist us in broadening and deepening our knowledge and understanding of them.

Viewed from this perspective, Gandhi was surely right. Allowing the cultures of all lands to be blown about our houses as freely as possible opens up a vast cornucopia of possibilities to solve our problems and enhance our lives. And refusing to be blown off our feet by any one culture prevents us from becoming shortsighted, narrow-minded, and from carrying things to extremes. What better place to do all this than in a city like Toronto, with its incredible mixture of different cultures and ethnic groups as well as its countless cultural resources and assets.

Chapter 11
Culture and Spirituality

I have had the good fortune to have been deeply immersed in culture in all its diverse forms and manifestations over the course of my life.

This immersion has enriched my life in many ways. It has made it possible for me to experience a great deal of joy, happiness, and fulfillment, learn a great deal about the many different cultures in the world, and achieve my basic goals and objectives. It has also enhanced my understanding of what is most valuable, essential, and worthwhile in life, as well as why I believe the transition to a cultural age in the future is so imperative. In addition, the more I have become immersed in culture, the more my life has become spiritual in nature.

Of course, there is no single path to spirituality. There are many, just as there are many paths to happiness, contentment, and fulfillment.

For millions of people, spirituality is achieved through religion and involvement in a specific religion and religious group. Not only is this the key to living a full, upright, and moral life, but also the key to experiencing higher levels of spirituality and possibly even encounters with the divine. Virtually all the different religions of the world—Buddhism, Hinduism, Islam, Christianity, Judaism, Sikhism, and so forth—believe that spirituality is achieved by making a strong commitment to the values, teachings, and beliefs of the faith and adhering to these values, teachings, and beliefs as fully as possible.

Others have a different take on this matter. They believe spirituality is achieved through meditation, mindfulness, the teachings of individuals such as Eckhart Tolle, Deepak Chopra, and Wayne Dyer, or the preaching of many evangelists, mystics, and others who possess strong convictions about spirituality and how it can be realized. This is also possible through involvement in many other activities, such as the arts, sciences, humanities, education, recreation, and appreciation and reverence for the natural environment.

To date, little consideration has been given to the role that culture can play in opening the doors to spirituality. This is probably because culture manifests itself in the world in many different ways—the arts, humanities, heritage of history, complex whole, total way of life, relationship with the natural environment, organizational forms of different species, and so forth[40]—and this causes confusion and misunderstanding for most people.

While many people see the different ways culture can be seen as a real liability, I see it as a powerful asset. This is because each of these "*manifestations of culture*" possesses the potential to open the doors to spirituality in one way or another, which will become apparent both from the personal experiences I have had with each of these manifestations over the years and from what many cultural scholars have had to say about this subject. This makes culture an ideal vehicle for achieving an enhanced sense of spirituality and countless other goals in life.

My first real encounter with spirituality was in the arts. This is not surprising given the fact that many people believe "the arts" and "culture" are synonymous. Moreover, it is well known that the arts possess the potential to lift people to incredible heights and transport them to ethereal places and spaces. As George Bernard Shaw said in *Back to Methuselah*, "you use a glass mirror to see your face; you use works of art to see your soul."

When I was young, my parents enrolled me in art classes at the Art Gallery of Toronto, now the Art Gallery of Ontario, arranged piano and singing lessons for me, and enrolled me in a choir at Grace Church on-the-Hill, as noted earlier. It wasn't long before I became aware of the intimate connection between the arts, culture, and spirituality, since many of these activities lifted me out of the commonplace and propelled me to very high heights.

Whether it was painting pictures, playing pieces on the piano, or singing hymns and anthems in the choir, I felt a certain awe come over me whenever I was engaged in any of these activities. This was especially true for singing in the choir, since a great deal of beautiful music was combined with exquisite architecture and an enormous amount of sacred liturgy and pageantry. I soon realized that spirituality is not confined to adults or people in their twilight years. It can be experienced at any age or in any walk in life, and often in profound, moving, and very powerful ways.

Awareness of the intimate connection between the arts, culture, and spirituality has broadened and deepened substantially in me over the years. Many musical compositions, plays, paintings, poems, architectural masterpieces, and the like produce spiritual feelings in me that border on the sublime and sometimes the divine.

If the arts provide an excellent example of the rich potential that culture possesses to open the doors to spirituality, so do the humanities and finer things in life. Many of the things that are included in this area—ethics, education, philosophy, jurisprudence, history, language, and so forth—as well as such values and virtues as the quest for peace, order, equality, and justice, the pursuit of knowledge, wisdom, beauty, and truth, and the importance of caring, sharing, cooperation, and compassion confirm this.

I often think of Mahatma Gandhi, Mother Teresa, and Dr. Martin Luther King Jr. when I reflect on these matters, largely because they led exemplary lives in numerous respects. Whenever I think of all the painful experiences they were forced to endure—and how the lives of Gandhi and King were snuffed out so quickly and brutally—I recall Dr. King's comment towards the end of his life that he wanted nothing more than to leave behind him a life totally committed to a cause.

If the arts, humanities, and finer things in life have a great deal to do with spirituality, so does the heritage of history. This is probably why many people think this heritage is one of culture's greatest assets and most precious gifts.

If I were able to travel backward or forward in time, I would definitely choose to travel backward. This is partly because I am not too excited about certain present and prospective developments—a Gothic cathedral does much more for me than a colossal office tower—but mostly because I am fascinated with the past and the magnificent legacy we have inherited from the past.

In addition to countless other things, this remarkable legacy includes the cultural accomplishments of all the diverse peoples of the world; all the world's greatest cities and historical sights—Venice with its enticing architecture and enchanting canals, Isfahan and Istanbul with their exquisite mosques, Kyoto with its ancient temples and Buenos Aires, Marrakech, and Savannah with their captivating streets and sumptuous squares; all the world's greatest achievements in the arts, sciences, religion, education, economics, medicine, philosophy, and the like; all the most powerful ideas, theories, and writings that have been created; and especially all the myriad cultures and civilizations that exist throughout the world, each with its own unique character and characteristics. Little wonder Jacob Burckhardt—the great Swiss cultural scholar who did so much to shed light on the Italian Renaissance and Greek and Roman classical culture—called this incredible gift "the silent promise" that possesses the potential to transform the entire past into a "spiritual possession."[41]

One institution that has taken Burckhardt's beliefs in this matter to heart is UNESCO. This organization has been steadily and systematically translating lofty ideals such as these into concrete realities for more than half a century. Not only does it place an extremely high priority on the tangible and intangible cultural heritage of humankind, including all the world heritage sites around the globe, but it also places an exceedingly high priority on preserving and protecting this priceless legacy and making it accessible to present and future generations.

We are the beneficiaries of this profuse and magnificent legacy of artefacts and accomplishments. This has become steadily more apparent as a result of major developments in communications and technology that make it possible for all people and all countries to enjoy cultural achievements from the past in all parts of the world. I get elated whenever I think that virtually every person, organization, country, and culture throughout the world now possesses the means to tap into these achievements no matter where they are situated.

In many ways, this is where matters stood for me with respect to culture and spirituality until I was in my late forties. My experiences in this area were limited largely to "*specific moments of spirituality*" that tended to happen when I was exposed to certain works of art, the finer things in life, and the legacy from the past. What I was not experiencing, however, was anything that might be considered a "*permanent state of spirituality.*"

Things started to change in this respect after a fortunate experience I had one day in the Bladen Library at the University of Toronto. I was in the library doing some research on culture—which had become my central concern and main passion in life by this time—when I came across a book by Sir Edward Burnett Tylor, one of the world's first anthropologists, called *The Origins of Culture*. There, staring me in the face on the very first page (as mentioned earlier), was Tylor's holistic definition of culture as "the complex whole" or "total way of life" of people and countries.

This definition struck me like a thunderbolt. I had long believed that there was far more to culture than the arts, humanities, finer things in life, and heritage of history—essential and fundamental as these are—because I had come across numerous references to many other activities that cultural scholars felt should also be included in culture. Here, at last, was confirmation of this.

While culture is not the only activity to be concerned with the complex whole or the total way of life of people and countries—these are also of concern in philosophy, religion, science, medicine, and other fields—I have been keenly interested in and committed to this all-encompassing way of seeing and dealing with culture ever since that fortuitous day in the Bladen Library. Most prominent in this regard are holism in general and the holistic perception and manifestation of culture and cultures in particular. Indeed, it would not be far off the mark to say that the whole, holism, and the holistic perception and manifestations of culture and cultures have together served as the guiding force and been the principal preoccupations in my life ever since.

Some may call what occurred in the Bladen Library that day an "epiphany," since it caused me to see and understand the world and life in a totally different way and an entirely new light. However, I would call it a "cultural transformation," since it helped me to see and understand the world, and the vast majority of things in the world, as they really are and not as they are presented to us as a result of specialization and our penchant for dividing the whole—and wholes—up into parts in order to study those parts in detail.

The implications of this for spirituality are clear and unequivocal. Focusing attention on the whole, wholes, holism, and the holistic understanding of culture and cultures has provided me with a much more all-encompassing and inclusive way of seeing and understanding reality and the world. It has also provided a gateway to living life on a much higher plane of existence.

From that point on, whenever I thought about other countries, other cultures, and the world at large, I thought about them as wholes and not merely smorgasbords of disconnected and unrelated pieces. My focus is always on the whole, and with it, what brings things together rather than splits them apart. This is especially true for people. I am fascinated with this because years earlier I came across several cultural scholars who had written about "*the whole person.*" While I tucked this information away in my mind at the time, it took on far greater significance and meaning when I became aware of the whole and holism as they relate to culture and people, and made a strong commitment to this way of thinking.

One of the scholars who wrote about the whole person in

terms of culture was Matthew Arnold, as noted earlier. John Cowper Powys had similar thoughts on this matter, although he expressed them in a slightly different way when he said, "The whole purpose and end of culture is a thrilling happiness of a particular sort—of the sort, in fact, that is caused by a response to life made by a harmony of the intellect, the imagination, and the senses."[42]

These insights were very helpful to me at the time because I was struggling to become a whole person and they emphasized how essential it is to achieve balance and harmony among all the diverse faculties and factors that constitute human beings and human nature: material and non-material; mind and body; work and leisure; egoism and altruism; the self and the other; and all the other dichotomous divisions that are associated with people and often used to describe them.

Thus far, little has been said in this chapter about the relationship between human beings and the natural environment, yet another manifestation of culture with profound implications for spirituality and the world of the future. The time has come to address this requirement, since an intimate connection exists between human beings, the natural environment, culture, and spirituality that must also be considered and taken into account.

Interestingly, culture's association with these matters can be traced back to classical times. This is because culture as a word and as an idea derives originally from the Latin verb "*colere*" meaning "to grow," "to till," and especially "to cultivate." This is the way Cicero, the Roman orator and statesman, used the word and the idea for the first time in history when he said "*cultura anima philosophia est*," which is usually translated as "*culture is the philosophy or cultivation of the soul.*" Interestingly, Herder expressed something similar to this many centuries later when he said, "The cultivation of a people is the flower of its existence."

This connection between culture, the natural environment, and spirituality is imperative and profound. Despite the fact that this connection has been largely ignored in the modern era and economic age, it explains why we have words in our vocabulary like agriculture, horticulture, silvaculture, viticulture, and many others that confirm that there has been an intimate relationship between human beings, culture, and the natural environment dating back more than two thousand years.

Many cultural and ecological scholars have written at length and very passionately about this relationship in recent years, including Arne Naess, Fritjof Capra, David Suzuki, George Sessions, James Lovelock, and many others. However, no scholars have written more compellingly about this relationship—and the dire need to transform it—than Brian Swimme and Thomas Berry. In books like *The Universe Story, Dream of the Earth*, and others, Swimme and Berry have made a convincing case for "deep ecology," as well as treating the natural environment as a "spiritual gift" in much that same way that Jacob Burckhardt made a powerful case for treating the heritage of history as a "spiritual possession."

All these perceptions of culture and various activities associated with them have helped to bring me closer to experiencing a permanent state of spirituality and not just specific moments of spirituality. They have also helped to open the doors to the final manifestaton of culture being considered here, namely the organizational forms and structures of different species, both human and non-human.

I have long been interested in the organizational forms and structures adopted by human beings and all the different cultures they have created and are creating, because they are so diverse, complex, intriguing, and sophisticated. This is largely because they are based on very different worldviews, values, customs, traditions, beliefs, and ways of life. As a result, some cultures are best known for their architectural accomplishments and culinary achievements—Chinese, Indian, French, Thai, and Turkish cultures, for example—whereas others are best known for their religious, industrial, and athletic capabilities, such as Buddhist, British, and American cultures. There is no single pattern or characteristic that fits all the many diverse cultures in the world. They are all different and unique in one way or another.

Lately, I have become fascinated with the organizational forms and structures of other species and the cultures they create. This is because their cultures are also wholes made up of many parts. The cultures of bees, ants, trees, and other species in the natural realm confirm the fact that animals and plants have cultures just as people do, and what is more, create them in much the same way as human beings.

Consider bees, for instance. The bee culture is also a whole composed of many different parts. This whole, with its well-defined system of queen, drone, and worker bees, its rigid hierarchy and division of labour, its finely-tuned communications networks and sensory capabilities, and its impressive productive capacities, acts to ensure the survival of bees as a species and guarantee a continuous supply of products. These products, such as honey, wax, the beehive, and the honeycomb, are much in demand in the human realm and have both a functional and aesthetic significance. The beehive and the honeycomb, for instance, are intricately designed and highly sophisticated cultural creations, comparable in their style, function, and complexity to many of the cultural creations created by human beings, even if they are far smaller in size and more elementary in character.

An even better example of this—and one much closer to the experience of human beings—is the cultures and cultural creations of elephants. It is a well-known fact that elephants have phenomenal memories—memories that may be even greater than the memories of human beings. However, what is becoming increasingly apparent as a result of contemporary research is the fact that elephants have highly complex and very sophisticated cultures—cultures that are predicated on a great deal of caring, sharing, intimacy, and compassion. Not only do elephants bond with each other in much the same way that human beings bond, but also they are each other's keepers in the sense that they look after each other very attentively when one of them is sick, elderly, in distress, or threatened in some way. Moreover, they look after their young in much the same way that people do, doting over them in countless ways and actively participating in their upbringing, training, education, and development.

What is true for elephants and bees is true for other animal species, even if in a less intense way and not to the same extent as human beings. Every species of animals has its own cultures and forms of cultural creation, including its distinctive methods of procreation, habitation, social bonding, community organization, networking, and consumption and production activity. This is not surprising in view of the fact that animals, like people, are living organisms, and, as such, obey the laws governing all living things.

And what is true for humans and other animals is also true for plants. As living organisms, they also have many needs and requirements, such as the need for food, water, air, and nutrients, birth, life, and death, consumption and elimination, communication and bonding with other plants, and so much more. In fact, recent research is revealing that the gap between human beings and plants is not as great as was once assumed. This is because plants, like people and animals, have feelings and emotions, experience pain, pleasure, and happiness, form communities, protect one another, have friendships, make connections, help each other in difficult times, and so forth. This is especially true for trees, as Peter Wohlleben points out in his informative book *The Hidden Life of Trees*: *What They Feel, How They Communicate*:

> If you look at roadside embankments, you might be able to see how trees connect with each other through their root systems. On these slopes, rain often washes away the soil, leaving the underground networks exposed.
>
> Scientists in the Harz mountains in Germany have discovered that this really is a case of interdependence, and most individual trees of the same species growing in the same stand are connected to each other through their root systems. It appears that nutrient exchange and helping neighbors in times of need is the rule, and this leads to the conclusion that forests are superorganisms with interconnections much like ant colonies.[43]

What does all this have to do with spirituality? Actually, a great deal. Culture and cultures are without doubt the highest forms of creation when they are looked at in holistic terms, regardless of whether they are created by human beings or by other species. This is because they are highly complex wholes made up of many different parts and there is little else in the world that can compare with them. This is why Alfred Kroeber and Clyde Kluckhohn, two American cultural scholars, said that "Culture constitutes the topmost phenomenal level yet recognized—or for that matter, now imaginable—in the realm of nature."[44] This is also why Jin Li said in her informative book *Cultural Foundations of Learning: East and West* when discussing the quintessential importance of culture for humans: "Culture, as the largest human created system (as opposed to our biology), penetrates so profoundly into all spheres of human life that it alters human cognition, emotion, and behaviour.... Culture is like the air we breathe; we are completely dependent on it."[45] And what is true for culture and human beings is equally true for culture and all other species as recent research is revealing and revealing very rapidly.

Like the incredible breakthroughs that are now occurring in science—findings that are also an essential part of culture as a whole and designed to broaden our knowledge and understanding of the smallest subatomic particles as well as deepen our awareness and appreciation of the universe as a whole—this most expansive manifestation of culture of all possesses the potential to produce ever higher levels of existence and states of consciousness with respect to virtually everything that exists in the human and natural realms. Whether these levels and states have to do with the divine is unknown at present and may only be revealed in the fullness of time, if at all. Nevertheless, this does not alter the fact that the organizational forms and structures of all the different species in the world have a great deal to do with spirituality and the sublime in profuse, profound, and fundamental ways.

And this brings us to the remarkable potential culture

possesses to open the doors to spirituality when it is considered in comprehensive terms. It possesses the potential to do this because culture can be perceived and manifests itself in the world in many different ways, and each of these ways has a great deal to do with spirituality in one form or another.

From the most beautiful works of art and the artistic manifestation of culture to all the diverse cultures in the world and all the organizational forms, structures, and cultural creations of different species, there is no doubt that culture possesses an awesome potential to act as the key to spirituality in much the same way the arts possess an incredible capacity to act as the gateway to culture, cultures, and a cultural age. This is because culture makes it possible to move horizontally as well as vertically—in breadth as well as in depth—across virtually every domain and activity that exists in the world, from the human to the non-human, the simple to the complex, the individual to the collective, the local to the global, and the mundane to the profound. As Barbara Ward asked many years ago when she observed that the main environmental insight is that all things are linked, "Where is the thread that will lead us through the maze?" It is now clear that culture is this thread.

And this is not all. While an important part of spirituality involves going "outside the self" in order to expand our awareness and consciousness of the external world, an equally important part of spirituality also involves going "inside the self" in order to become much more aware, conscious, and acquainted with the internal world. In the final analysis, this is what is required to become a whole person, to "live in the whole, in the good, in the beautiful" as Goethe proposed and to "follow one's bliss" as Joseph Campbell advocated, and to achieve balance and harmony between and among all the diverse factors, forces, and faculties that constitute development and life.

This is important because it will not only bring people a great deal more fulfillment and happiness in life, it will also reduce the colossal demands that are being made on the natural environment and make it possible to walk more lightly on the land. This is because a much better balance will be achieved between people's material and non-material requirements. This is imperative if humanity is to come to grips with the difficult and debilitating problems that exist in the world today.

No challenge is greater in this respect than the need to come to grips with the continuous march of human numbers compared to the finite carrying capacity of the earth. In recent years, it has become apparent that the world's current population of 7.8 billion is exerting tremendous pressure on the natural environment, the globe's scarce resources, and the lives of other species. Given this fact, and the fact that world population is expected to increase in the years and decades ahead, there is no doubt that major environmental catastrophes are inevitable if humanity does not bring its material appetites under control and reduce its huge ecological footprint. Already, climate change and its manifestations such as global warming, the increased frequency of floods, hurricanes, droughts, and forest fires, and the devastation of coastal areas are revealing that severe consequences are in store for humanity if it persists in this practice.

Clearly much more emphasis will have to be placed on humanity's internal and non-material—rather than external and material—requirements if these and other problems are to be dealt with effectively. Hence the need for a quantum leap in the spiritual and qualitative side of life compared to the material and quantitative side. In global terms, a leap of this magnitude would bring about a great deal more environmental conservation while simultaneously making it possible for people to live on a much higher plane of existence and experience a great deal more spirituality in life. It will also bring about far more caring and sharing in the world, thereby reducing the severe income inequalities and social inequities and injustices that exist throughout the world today.

And this brings me back to my own situation and the personal experiences I have had with spirituality over the years. Each of the experiences I have had with the main manifestations of culture—from the arts, humanities, and heritage of history to the complex whole, the organizational forms and structures of all different species, and interactions with nature and the natural environment—has enriched my life in countless ways and made it possible for me to move progressively from specific moments of spirituality to something much closer to a permanent state of spirituality.

I am not there yet, but feel I am moving in the right direction in this regard. I have the sense that my growing awareness of culture and the cultural way of life is slowly but surely being transformed into a spiritual way of life. I hope this is the case, since culture is without doubt one of the best vehicles of all for opening the doors to spirituality and unlocking the secrets of the sublime and possibly even the divine.

Chapter 12

The Age of Culture: Why, What, and How

Culture in the future is the crux of the future.
Eleanora Barbieri Masini[46]

We have arrived at a crucial point in history. We can continue living in the economic age we are living in at present, or we can change direction and enter a cultural age in the future. The decision is ours to make.

It is not difficult to see why such a decision is necessary. Many complex, debilitating, and dangerous problems have emerged in the world in recent years that threaten humanity's well-being and indeed its very survival, including worsening shortages of natural resources and basic foodstuffs, huge disparities in income and wealth, conflicts between different genders, groups, races, religions, countries, and cultures, and the perpetual threat of nuclear, chemical, or biological warfare. Bringing matters to a head as this book was being finished were the threat of climate change and other environmental crises, the COVID-19 pandemic, and mass protests against racial prejudice and oppression occurring around the world. It doesn't take a psychic to predict how devastating all these problems could become if they are not dealt with effectively.

When the world's population was much smaller than it is today, there were enough resources to go around, weather conditions were more stable, and there was less human interaction, pollution, congestion, and waste. However, even then there were signs that humanity could be in for a rocky ride in the future, and Thomas Robert Malthus predicted that population growth would eventually outstrip the food supply and the means of subsistence.

Fortunately, an event had occurred half a century before Malthus' prediction that was destined to have a much more positive and powerful effect on the world. It was the publication of Adam Smith's book *The Wealth of Nations* in 1776. This event triggered a series of developments over the next 250 years that have had a profound global impact. Smith demonstrated in theoretical and practical terms how people's and countries' standards of living and quality of life could be increased significantly through various economic principles and modes of organization, including specialization and the pursuit of individuals' own self-interests.

These beliefs were strengthened when David Ricardo contended that economics should take precedence over politics and all other activities in society and constitute the principal preoccupation of countries and governments. They were strengthened even more when Karl Marx claimed that history should be interpreted in economic terms because every society is divisible into an "economic base" and a "non-economic superstructure," with economics the "cause" and "basis" of everything in society. For Marx, the economic interpretation of history was true not only in all places, but also for all times—past, present, and future. Marx's viewpoint was never seriously challenged; it was decided by the world's most powerful leaders and countries (even those that did not adopt what we now think of as "Marxist" economic systems) that Marx had uncovered a fundamental and universal truth. As a result, other interpretations of history and thoughts and ideas about future directions for humanity and the world were ignored. The central task now was to flesh out the economic interpretation in theoretical and practical terms and operationalize it.

This is largely what has happened in the world since the time of Marx. Economic ideas and activities are now accorded by far the highest priority in the world. This has been achieved by creating a comprehensive system of economic theory and practice, as well as developing a set of quantitative indicators—such as gross domestic product (GDP), per capita income, the rate of economic growth, and others—that measure economic progress and performance with scientific precision. These indicators are now the principal preoccupation of all countries, governments, corporations, citizens, and the world as a whole, especially after the theories of John Maynard Keynes and the Keynesians were implemented before, during, and after the Great Depression and the Second World War and served to further bolster the global economic system.

In recent years, this system has expanded its reach from the western world to the entire world, through the process known as "globalization." As a result of these occurrences, and others, we are now living in an economic age, one in which the development of economics and economies is the centrepiece of municipal, regional, national, and international affairs. It is now generally accepted everywhere in the world that if we look after economic matters properly, everything else will fall into place and work out for the best.

This reality is now so powerful and pervasive that it is impossible to call the present age anything but an economic age[47]—an age focused on producing as many goods and services and as much monetary wealth as possible. In order to do this, production, consumption, productivity, growth, and profits must be maximized and most activities must be valued primarily—if not exclusively—for their economic impact.

Humanity is now so deeply immersed in this age that its pre-eminence is taken for granted—at least until rather recently. During the last few decades, research undertaken by many scientific, environmental, governmental, and other organizations, as well as the findings of the Brundtland Commission on the Environment, the UN Intergovernmental Panel on Climate Change, and numerous other commissions, institutions, and agencies have caused some people to voice serious reservations about the economic age we are living in. Others have concluded that the status quo is not acceptable because the risks and dangers are too great. And still others feel that things must change and change substantially if environmental sustainability and human welfare, well-being, and equality are to be assured in the future.

Given this situation, a candid and impartial assessment of the economic age is imperative.[48] It is impossible to conduct this assessment without admitting that the economic age is by far humanity's greatest achievement to date. Not only has it resulted in the production, distribution, and consumption of vast quantities of goods and services and creation of immense material and monetary wealth, but it has also improved living standards and the quality of life for billions of people throughout the world since its beginnings in 1776. It has also contributed to countless advances in agriculture, industry, science, technology, education, communications, medicine, politics, the arts, and a great deal else. As a result, it is tempting to conclude that the economic age should continue indefinitely.

However, there are a number of problems with the economic age that must be addressed because they are evolving at a rapid rate and threatening to escalate out of control. The most obvious of these is the devastating effect the economic age is having on the natural environment. What makes this problem so acute, dangerous, and potentially life-threatening is the fact that throughout the entire duration of the economic age, the natural environment has been downplayed or ignored. It is impossible to insert the natural environment into the ideological underpinnings and basic principles and practices of the economic age *after the fact*. The architectural equivalent of the economic age and its neglect of environmental realities would be building a colossal office tower on sand or mud. The economic age rests on faulty foundations. At some point, it is bound to collapse. This fact is sufficient in and of itself to lead us to conclude that a very different kind of age is required in the future, one with new theoretical and practical underpinnings.

As difficult as this problem with the economic age is, it is not the only one. As time marches on, it becomes more and more apparent that the economic age is not capable of coming to grips with most of the other complex problems that exist in the world today, especially climate change, conflict among races, peoples, groups, religions, countries, and cultures, the spread of infectious diseases, vast inequalities in income and wealth, increased violence and terrorism, refugee and migration issues, countless communications and technological challenges, and the overall inability to achieve humanity's most important goals and maintain its highest ideals. This is because the economic age is designed for one thing, to create wealth, and not to deal with problems as vast, vital, debilitating, and multidimensional as these.

Despite this, the biggest problem of all with the age of economics is that economics is seen and treated as "the whole" and everything else is seen and treated as a "part of the whole" and consequently *part of economics*. But the truth is that *economics is not the whole*, regardless of how important it may be. There is a huge difference between saying that economics plays a crucial role in our lives and in the world, which is an undeniable fact, and saying that economics is the whole and everything else is part of it. There are many things in life and the world that have little or nothing to do with economics, such as friendship, love, compassion, companionship, trust, integrity, values, and truth.

This problem of what is "the whole" and what are "the parts of the whole" is the biggest challenge facing humanity. It affects everybody and everything. Since the whole is greater than the parts and the sum of the parts, humanity must be exceedingly careful about what it considers to be the whole and how it chooses to deal with this whole in the years ahead.

A great deal of light was shed on these matters when anthropologists began travelling to different parts of the world in the nineteenth and twentieth centuries to study human societies and behaviour in depth and on the ground. These researches led Edward Burnett Tylor to define culture as "the complex whole" or "total way of life" of people and countries, and anthropologists used this definition to describe and explain the holistic processes and phenomena they found during their studies. Since that time, the validity of regarding culture in this all-encompassing, holistic sense has been confirmed by countless anthropologists, sociologists, and cultural historians. Wole Soyinka, the African Nobel laureate in literature, views culture as the source from which all things flow and to which all things return, as indeed do most people when they speak of being "products of their culture."

What is true for culture in the general sense is also true for specific cultures, which are also wholes or total ways of life made up of countless parts. Seen from this holistic perspective, it is clear that the world is made up of culture and cultures at its core and in its fundamental essence. Like culture, cultures are also concerned with the complex whole or total way of life of peoples and countries and therefore how those peoples and countries visualize and interpret the world, organize themselves, conduct their affairs, embellish and enrich life, position themselves in the world, and act in the world. Indeed, there is very little in the world that is not concerned with or connected to cultures in this all-inclusive sense. This is confirmed by the many ways "culture" and "cultures" have been seen and defined throughout history and manifest themselves in the world today.[49]

Such an all-encompassing perception of culture and cultures is desperately needed in the world of the present and the future. It is required to focus attention on the "big picture," since this is the one thing that is most lacking and urgently needed in the world today. It is also needed to bring people and activities together rather than to split them apart—*to unite rather than divide*—since doing so is what holism and the holistic perspective are really all about. Moreover, it is needed to make the changes that are necessary in people's lives, behaviour, worldviews, and lifestyles to come to grips with the environmental crisis and other problems, because these problems have a great deal to do with culture and cultures as ways of life and the dire need to change them. And finally, it is needed to situate economics and economies properly in a much broader and deeper cultural and environmental context. This will ensure that the development of all the diverse economies in the world is informed by environmental, social, ethical, medical, and human values and not only commercial, financial, and technological interests, and are therefore clean, green, shared, sustainable, and most of all, humane.

Unfortunately, the holistic perception of culture and cultures has been ignored over the last few centuries because humanity has been preoccupied with economics, economies, specialization, and economic growth. However, this all-encompassing perception must now be fully realized, embraced, and utilized because of its profound implications and powerful consequences for all decisions, developments, policies, and actions in the world. As Ruth Benedict, the American cultural scholar, said, "The whole *determines* the parts, not only their relation, but their very nature."

What is true for the holistic perception of culture and cultures is also true for the works of cultural scholars. While these works have been largely ignored outside the cultural domain over the last 250 years because of humanity's preoccupation with economics, they have a great deal of significance for the world at present and its development in the future. For just as economics has its "giants" such as Adam Smith, David Ricardo, Karl Marx, Alfred Marshall, John Maynard Keynes, and others, so culture has its giants as well—Voltaire, Jacob Burckhardt, Matthew Arnold, Edward Burnett Tylor, Johan Huizinga, Alfred Kroeber, Ruth Benedict, Margaret Mead, Pitirim Sorokin, Raymond Williams, Edward T. Hall, Joseph Campbell, and many others. It is regrettable that the contributions of these and other cultural scholars have been neglected outside the cultural realm for such a long time because they embody an immense reservoir of knowledge, wisdom, insight, and understanding, as well as inspiring values, ideas, and ideals that are germane to the world situation and human condition at present and going forward into the future.

The time has come to capitalize on the holistic perception of culture and cultures and the rich legacy of thoughts, ideas, and ideals bequeathed to us by generations and indeed centuries of cultural scholars. Not only is this vital to addressing some of the world's most debilitating, acute, and life-threatening problems, but it is also the key to making the transition from the economic age to a cultural age. It is through ever deeper forays into the domain of the arts, culture, cultures, and legacy of cultural scholars that a portrait of an age of this type emerges and begins to manifest itself in the world.

It is a portrait that starts with people, as well it should. For all people live a "cultural life" in the sense that they are compelled to combine all the different parts of their lives—economic, social, religious, political, educational, artistic, recreational, spiritual, and so forth—to form a whole or total way of life. Regardless of what priorities they assign to specific activities in their lives—economics, religion, education, politics, the arts, the sciences, or sports, for instance—as well as what their specific worldviews, values, beliefs, and lifestyles might be, the fact remains that all the activities they are involved in must be woven together to create a holistic entity and comprehensive whole.

Developing harmony and balance between and among all these activities is what living a cultural life and living in a cultural age are really all about. Not only is this required to experience a great deal more joy, happiness, and fulfillment in life, but it is also needed to enjoy good health, well-being, spirituality, contentment, and the experience of the sublime. What makes this so important is the fact that if this balance and harmony are not achieved, disharmonies and imbalances set in and compound over time—disharmonies and imbalances that are inimical rather than conducive to a better state of affairs and a more satisfying way of life for present and future generations.

This is what makes the research, publications, findings, and conferences of the Scientific Research Institute of Spiritual Development of Man and the International UNESCO Chair in "Spiritual and Cultural Values of Upbringing and Education" at Volodymyr Dahl East Ukrainian National University so valuable and timely. Scholars associated with this institution have been researching and writing about how people's personalities and lives can be developed and enriched through the arts, sciences, culture, and spirituality for several decades now. In so doing, they have provided keen insights into what is required to prepare young people and future generations for life in a cultural age, as well as the inspiration and leadership qualities that are required to enter this age and enable it to flourish.

What makes their work in this area particularly valuable is the fact that there is a great deal to be learned from how people live their lives and cultivate their personalities that is relevant to the development, functioning, and flourishing of cultures in the all-inclusive sense. This was why Ruth Benedict believed that cultures are really "personalities writ large" because both cultures and personalities are wholes or total ways of life made up of many different parts. To progress further in this area, it is necessary to turn to the arts, artists, and arts organizations because they create many of the signs, symbols, ideas, insights, ideals, and works that are required to act as gateways and open the doors to culture, all the diverse cultures in the world, and a cultural age. Paintings, plays, music, stories, dances, films, myths, legends, metaphors, culinary achievements, architectural masterpieces, and other works of art are elements of cultures that have a deep symbolic significance for all cultures. Think, for instance, of what Sibelius' *Finlandia* with its stirring melodies, Smetana's *Moldau* with its rapidly flowing sounds of water, Copland's *Appalachian Spring* with its *Simple Gifts*, and Monet's *Water Lilies* with its exquisite flowers mean to the people and cultures of Finland, the Czech Republic, the United States, and France. Mahatma Gandhi captured this best when he said that "a nation's culture resides in the hearts and in the soul of its people."

Regardless of what cultures we are concerned with, the challenge is the same for cultures as it is for people—to achieve balance and harmony between many different parts. This highlights one of the most fundamental differences between the age of economics and the age of culture. In the age of economics, the focus is on developing economics and economies in breadth and depth *as parts*. In the age of culture, the focus is on developing culture and cultures in depth and breadth *as wholes*, but equally importantly, if not more so, *achieving balance and harmony between and among the many different parts of these wholes.*

Just as it is necessary to achieve balance and harmony *within* cultures—as well as *between* cultures, it must be quickly added—so it is necessary to position cultures effectively in the natural, historical, and global environment. Not only will this result in greater environmental sustainability, but it will also make it possible to come to grips with the cultural baggage we inherit from the past and carry with us in the present and the future. This is the key to reducing conflicts and improving relations between the diverse peoples, races, countries, and cultures of the world, as well as ensuring that all cultures are properly situated in time as well as in space.

It follows from everything that has been said here about the age of culture that this age would not be an alternative to the economic age. Rather, it would *incorporate* the economic age—along with a great deal else—in a much broader, deeper, and more compelling and all-encompassing vision of the human condition, the global situation, and the world of the future. It is a vision that is much more in keeping with the needs of all people, countries, and species. Possibly this is what Erasmus had in mind when, early in the modern era, he declared, "What a world I see dawning before me," or what Eleanora Barbieri Masini meant when she said, "Culture in the future is the crux of the future."

It is impossible to discuss the need for and nature of a cultural age without considering how this age can actually be achieved. In order to do this, it is necessary to examine the roles and responsibilities of the three principal participants in the creation and development of such an age: people and organizations working in the cultural field, governments, and the general public.

Unfortunately, people and organizations working in the cultural field are at present very diffuse and disconnected. This is because they are spread across many different disciplines and fields—all the various art forms, the heritage of history, cultural industries, cultural studies, anthropology, sociology, ecology, and biology—with little or no communication or connection between them. Nevertheless, these people and organizations are the most important of all because they are deeply committed to the prominent role culture needs to play in the world, and they must therefore provide the leadership and inspiration that are required to move the arts, culture, and cultures in general—and arts and cultural development and policy in particular—out of the margins and into the mainstream in order to usher in a cultural age as the next great epoch in human history.

They also have a responsibility for providing the educational materials, resources, courses, and curricula that are necessary to broaden, deepen, and enrich our knowledge and understanding of the intricacies and complexities of culture and cultures as wholes or total ways of life in both theoretical and practical terms, to improve relations between the diverse cultures and civilizations of the world, and to enhance awareness of the dangers and shortcomings of culture and cultures and not just their strengths, assets, and benefits. Moreover, they must also increase appreciation and use of the tangible and intangible cultural heritage of humankind, as well as create the links, connections, bridges, networks, platforms, podcasts, algorithms, and artificial intelligence capabilities that are necessary to coalesce this group into a cohesive "cultural community" committed to espousing the best in human nature, conduct, and character, as well as reducing violence, conflict, systemic racism, and hate in the world.

Governments have the next most important role to play. Their responsibilities can be achieved by embracing the holistic perspective and integrative potential of culture. If this perspective and potential are not adopted by governments they will not be adopted at all, since governments, culture, and politics are capable of embodying and acting upon one of humanity's greatest ideals, namely the need to act in the best interests of *all* people, countries, and the world as a whole, not just in the best interests of *some* people, countries, and only certain parts of the world. If governments do not act in such a way, the transition to a cultural age will not occur.

And this brings us to the general public, which could end up playing the greatest role of all in ushering in a cultural age if people focus their attention, energies, and priorities on achieving culture's highest and wisest ideals. Most notable in this regard are promoting peace, order, justice, equality, and spirituality in the world, as well as making it possible for all people and all countries to enjoy reasonable standards of living and a decent quality of life without straining the world's scarce resources and finite carrying capacity to the breaking point. To do so would be to make an indispensable contribution to the realization of a cultural age at a crucial time in the history of the world.

Relevant Books and Articles by D. Paul Schafer

Books

Arguments for the Arts: Towards a Dynamic and Innovative Arts Policy. Scarborough, Ont.: Arts Scarborough, 1982.

Culture: Beacon of the Future. Westport, Conn.: Praeger, 1998.

The Challenge of Cultural Development. Markham, Ont.: World Culture Project, 1994.

Revolution or Renaissance: Making the Transition from an Economic Age to a Cultural Age. Ottawa: University of Ottawa Press, 2008.

The Age of Culture. Oakville, Ont.: Rock's Mills Press, 2014.

The Secrets of Culture. Oakville, Ont.: Rock's Mills Press, 2015.

The Cultural Personality. Oakville, Ont.: Rock's Mills Press, 2018.

Articles

"Towards a New World Order: The Age of Culture." *UNESCO Cultures* 2: 3 (1975).

"The Age of Culture: Prospects and Implications." *UNESCO Cultures* 2: 4 (1975).

"The Culturescape: Self-Awareness of Communities." *UNESCO Cultures* 5: 1 (1978).

"Culture and Cosmos: The Role of Culture in the World of the Future." *UNESCO Cultures* 7: 2 (1980).

"Culture and the New World Order." *Proceedings of the Conference on the New International Economic Order: Philosophical Basis and Socio-cultural Implications.*

Vienna: International Progress Organization, 1980.

"The Cultural Interpretation of History: Beacon of the Future." Reprinted in part in *The Future of the Past: Historical Identity and Permanence and Change*. Buffalo, N.Y.: Center for Integrative Studies; Durango, Col.: Center of Southwest Studies; Mexico City: Center for Economic and Social Studies of the Third World; and Paris: UNESCO, 1980. Reprinted in full in Robin Blazer and Robert Dunham, eds., *Arts and Reality: A Casebook of Concern*. Introduction by Northrop Frye. Vancouver: Talon Books, 1986.

"The New World Order: A Contribution to the World Decade for Cultural Development." *Major Programme I: Reflection on World Problems and Future Oriented Studies*. Paris: UNESCO, 1989.

"Culture: Beacon of the Future." *Razvoj Development International* 6: 2–3 (1991). Published by the Institute for Development and International Relations, Zagreb, Croatia.

"The Evolution and Character of the Concept of Culture." *World Futures: The Journal of General Evolution* 38: 4 (1993).

"Culture as It Might Be." *Futures: The Journal of Forecasting, Planning and Policy* 26: 1 (1994).

"Cultures and Economies: Irresistible Forces Encounter Immovable Objects." *Futures: The Journal of Forecasting, Planning and Policy* 26: 8 (1994).

"Towards a New World System: A Cultural Perspective." *Futures: The Journal of Forecasting, Planning and Policy* 28: 3 (1996).

"The Millennium Challenge: Making the Transition from an 'Economic Age' to a 'Cultural Age.'" *World Futures: The Journal of General Evolution* 51 (1998).

"A New Model of Development for the New Millennium." *World*

Futures: The Journal of General Evolution 55 (2000).

"Culture and Cultures: Key Learning Requirements for the Future." Published online as a chapter in a book on learning communities at http://www.creatinglearningcommunities.org (2001).

"The Arts in Turbulent Times." *The Artspaper* 11: 1 (2001).

"The Arts and Cities." *The Artspaper* 12: 3 (2002).

"Diversity and Sustainable Development: Contemporary Concerns or Permanent Realities?" *Culturelink* Special Issue (2002/2003) on "Cultural Diversity and Sustainable Development." Published by Culturelink and the Institute for International Relations, Zagreb, Croatia, 2003.

"A New System of Politics: Government, Governance, and Political Decision-making in the Twenty-first Century." *World Futures: The Journal of General Evolution* 61: 7 (2005).

"Feasting on Cultures to Solve Our Problems and Enrich Our Lives." Posted in 2006 in the "Hot Topics" section of the World Culture Project website. http://www3.sympatico.ca/dpaulschafer.

"The New Politics: Government and Governance in the Twenty-first Century." *Humanitad World Leadership Magazine*, no. 1 (2006). Published in London.

"The Cultural Imperative: The Role of Culture in the World of the Future." Posted in 2010 in the "Hot Topics" section of the World Culture Project website.

"A Cultural Model of Development." Posted in 2010 in the "Hot Topics" section of the World Culture Project website.

"The Future of Culture." Posted in 2010 in the "Hot Topics" section of the World Culture Project website.

"Foundations for Life." Collection of research materials.

"Spirituality of a Personality: Methodology, Theory and Practice," Issue 1 (42), 2011, Scientific Research Institute of Spiritual Development of Man and UNESCO Chair on Spiritual Cultural Values of Upbringing and Education, Volodymyr Dahl East Ukrainian National University, 2012, pp. 178–193.

"Culture and Spirituality: Key to Life and Living in the Twenty-first Century." Collection of research materials. "Spirituality of a Personality: Methodology, Theory and Practice," Issue 1 (54) 2013, Scientific Research Institute of Spiritual Development of Man and UNESCO Chair on Spiritual Cultural Values of Upbringing and Education, Volodymyr Dahl East Ukrainian National University, 2013, pp. 3–21.

Culture and Spirituality: Key to Life and Living in the Twenty-first Century. Critical Orientations to Sustainability and Spirituality, The Global Centre for the Study of Sustainable Futures and Spirituality, Public Media Agency Sdn Bhd, Petaling Jaya, Selangor, Malaysia, 2014.

"Living a Cultural Life." Collection of research materials. "Spirituality of a Personality: Methodology, Theory and Practice" in support of UNESCO's 70th Anniversary Celebrations, Issue 1 (64) 2015, Institute of Spiritual Development of Man and UNESCO Chair on Spiritual Cultural Values of Upbringing and Education, Volodymyr Dahl East Ukrainian National University in 2015, pp. 283–306.

"Creating a World System Conducive to the Flourishing of Culture and Spirituality." Collection of research materials. "Spirituality of a Personality: Methodology, Theory and Practice" in support of UNESCO's 70th Anniversary Celebrations, Issue 1 (65) 2015, Scientific Research Institute of Spiritual Development of Man and UNESCO Chair on Spiritual Cultural Values of Upbringing and Education, Volodymyr Dahl East Ukrainian National University in 2015.

"The Arts: Key to a Full and Fulfilling Cultural Life." Collection of research materials. "Spirituality of a Personality: Methodology, Theory and Practice," Materials of the VII International Scientific and Practical Conference "Spiritual Image of Man of Culture of the Twenty-First Century, Methodology, Theory and Practice," May 24, 2016, Kyiv, Issue 3 (72), Scientific Research Institute of Spiritual Development of Man and UNESCO Chair on Spiritual Cultural Values of Upbringing and Education, Volodymyr Dahl East Ukrainian National University, Ukraine, 2016.

"The Case for Culture," posted to the websites of League Cultural Diplomacy (*Where Words Fail*), International Institute for Gastronomy, Art, Culture and Tourism, Society for Education Through Art, and Center of Ecozoic Studies, *Musings* in 2017.

"The Role of Music in the Development of the Human and Cultural Personalities," Collection of research materials. "Spirituality of a Personality: Methodology, Theory and Practice," Materials of the IX International Scientific and Practical Conference "Cultural Personality in the Light of Upbringing, Education, and Spiritual Security," May 23, 2018, Kyiv, Issue 2 (83), Part 1. Scientific Research Institute of Spiritual Development of Man and UNESCO Chair on Spiritual Cultural Values of Upbringing and Education, Volodymyr Dahl East Ukrainian National University, Ukraine, 2018.

"The Age of Culture: Why, What, and How?" Collection of research materials. "Spirituality of a Personality: Methodology, Theory and Practice," Materials of the X International Scientific and Practical Conference "Spiritual and Cultural Upbringing of a Personality in Conditions of Humanity's Entry into the Age of Culture" within the Framework of D. Paul Schafer's International Project "The Age of Culture," May 30, 2019, Kyiv, Issue 2 (89), part 1. Scientific Research Institute of Man and UNESCO Chair on Spiritual Cultural Values of Upbringing and Education, Volodymyr Dahl East Ukrainian National University, Ukraine, 2019.

Out of the Economic Age and into a Cultural Age, 48-minute video posted on YouTube, November, 2019.

"The Future of Arts Education: Broaden, Deepen, Diversify, Intensify," to be included in a special collection of articles on arts education and published by the Scientific Research Institute of Spiritual Development of Man and UNESCO Chair on Spiritual and Cultural Values of Upbringing and Education, Volodymyr Dahl East Ukrainian National University in Ukraine, 2020.

Endnotes

1. Robert Redfield, *The Little Community: Viewpoints for the Study of a Human Whole* (Chicago: University of Chicago Press, 1973), p. 161.
2. Charles R. Joy (ed.), *Albert Schweitzer: An Anthology* (Boston: The Beacon Press, 1947), p. 131.
3. C. P. Snow, *The Two Cultures and the Scientific Revolution* (Cambridge: Cambridge University Press, 1959). This book was published following C. P. Snow's Rede Lecture on this subject earlier in 1959.
4. C. P. Snow, *The Two Cultures and a Second Look: An Expanded Version of* The Two Cultures and the Scientific *Revolution* (New York: New American Library, 1963).
5. In recent years, a broader version of STEM has emerged in some parts of the world. It is called STEAM, and is designed to include the Arts along with Science, Technology, Engineering, and Mathematics in a broader and deeper approach to some of the most important aspects of education and learning for present and future generations.
6. D. Paul Schafer and Sal Amenta, "Image of the Educated Person of the Future." Paper prepared at the request of the International Bureau of Education in Geneva for distribution at its 43rd Conference on Education in 1992.
7. D. Paul Schafer, *Revolution or Renaissance: Making the Transition from an Economic Age to a Cultural Age* (Ottawa: University of Ottawa Press, 2008).
8. D. Paul Schafer, *The Cultural Personality* (Oakville, Ont.: Rock's Mills Press, 2018).
9. Findings like this have also been confirmed by the International Laboratory for Brain, Music, and Sound

Research, which was created to "study music as a portal into the most complex aspects of human brain functions." This is also true of the many studies undertaken by Jonathan Burdette, a neuroradiologist at Wake Forest Baptist Medical Center, who has concluded that "[i]t doesn't matter if it's Bach, the Beatles, Brad Paisley, or Bruno Mars. Your favorite music likely triggers a similar type of activity in your brain as other people's favorites do in theirs."

10. Information on these and many other studies and findings related to the impact of the arts in general and arts education in particular, and especially the functioning of the minds, brains, and thoughts of artists, can be accessed on The Healing Power of Arts and Artists website.
11. Lewis Mumford, *The Culture of Cities* (New York: Harcourt, Brace and World, Inc., 1938), p. 6.
12. Amos Rapoport, "Culture and the Urban Order," in John A. Agnew, John Mercer and David E. Sopher (eds.), *The City in Cultural Context* (Boston: Allen and Unwin, 1984), p. 54.
13. Colin Mercer (guest ed.), *Convergence, Creative Industries and Civil Society: The New Cultural Policy, CULTURELINK*, Special Issue, 2001 (Zagreb: Institute for International Relations, 2001). Also see: Charles Landry, *The Creative City: A Toolkit for Urban Innovators* (London: Earthscan Publications Ltd., 2000); and Don Adams and Arlene Goldbard, *Creative Community: The Art of Cultural Development* (New York: The Rockefeller Foundation, 2001).
14. Bill Schiller, "Miracle in streets of Philadelphia: America's mayor spins gold from debt and decay," *The Toronto Star*, February 23, 2002, pp. A1, A26, A27.
15. Charles Landry, "A Cultural Approach to Developing the

Creative City," in *CULTURELINK*, vol. 11, no. 32, November 2000 (Zagreb: Institute for International Relations, 2000), p. 21.

16. Paul J. Braisted, *Cultural Cooperation: Keynote of the Coming Age*, The Hazen Pamphlets, Number 8 (New Haven: The Edward W. Hazen Foundation, 1945), pp. 5–6.
17. James Feibleman, *The Theory of Human Culture* (New York: Humanities Press, 1968), pp. 326–327.
18. Fritjof Capra, *Uncommon Wisdom: Conversations with Remarkable People* (New York: Simon and Schuster, 1988), p. 232.
19. R. King (ed.), *Goethe on Human Creativeness and Other Goethe Essays* (Athens, Georgia: University of Georgia Press, 1960), p. 236.
20. Alexander King, "Technological Determinants and Educational Needs of Society in Transition," in *Razvoj Development International*, vol. 5., no. 2 (July–December 1990), p. 199.
21. D. Paul Schafer, *The Character of Culture* (Scarborough, Ont.: World Culture Project, 1989).
22. UNESCO, *Mexico Declaration on Cultural Policies* (Paris: UNESCO, 1982).
23. UNESCO, *A Practical Guide to the World Decade for Cultural Development 1988-1997* (Paris: UNESCO, 1987), p. 16.
24. D. Paul Schafer, "The Cultural Interpretation of History: Beacon of the Future," in Robin Blaser and Robert Dunham (eds.), *Art and Reality: A Casebook of Concern*, introd. Northrop Frye (Vancouver: Talonbooks, 1986), pp. 167–187.
25. Rabindranath Tagore, as quoted in Paul J. Braisted,

Cultural Cooperation: Keynote to the Coming Age, The Hazen Pamphlets, Number 8 (New Haven: The Edward W. Hazen Foundation, 1945), p. 5.

26. Hugh Jenkins, *The Culture Gap: An Experience of Government and the Arts* (London: Marion Boyers, 1979), p. 10.
27. Karl J. Weintraub, *Visions of Culture: Voltaire, Guizot, Burckhardt, Lamprecht, Huizinga, Ortega y Gasset* (Chicago: University of Chicago Press, 1966), p. 216.
28. The World Decade for Cultural Development and the World Commission for Culture and Development were created in 1988 and 1993 respectively. The aims of the Decade were to ensure that the cultural dimension was taken into consideration in all economic development planning; to assist in the preservation and enrichment of cultural identity, including promotion of the arts and safeguarding of the national heritage; to broaden participation in cultural activity; and to foster international cultural cooperation. The aims of the Commission were to broaden and deepen understanding of culture and cultures and the way culture and cultures function throughout the world. See *Our Creative Diversity: Report of the World Commission on Culture and Development* (Paris: EGOPRIM, 1995).
29. See D. Paul Schafer, *Culture: Beacon of the Future* (Westport, Connecticut: Praeger, 1998), chapter 2, for a detailed analysis of the many different concepts and definitions of culture that have evolved over the course of history and are in use throughout the world today.
30. Edward Burnett Tylor, *The Origins of Culture* (New York: Harper and Row, 1958), p.1 (emphasis and insert mine).
31. Wole Soyinka, "Culture, Memory, and Development,"

International Conference on Culture and Development in Africa, April 2-3, 1992 (Washington: The World Bank, 1992), p. 21.

32. Schafer, *Culture: Beacon of the Future*, p. 40.
33. Mircea Malitza, "Culture and the New World Order: A Pattern of Integration," *Cultures*, vol. 3, no. 4 (Paris: UNESCO Press and La Baconnière, 1976), p. 102.
34. Giles Gunn, *The Culture of Criticism and the Criticism of Culture* (New York: Oxford University Press, 1987), p. 95.
35. Rapoport, "Culture and the Urban Order," p. 51.
36. Jere Paul Surber, *Culture and Critique: An Introduction to the Critical Discourses of Cultural Studies* (Boulder, Col.: Western Press, 1998), p. 238.
37. King (ed.), *Goethe on Human Creativeness*, p. ix.
38. UNESCO, *Our Creative Diversity: Report of the World Commission on Culture and Development* (Paris: UNESCO, 1995), p. 73.
39. Thelma Barer-Stein, *You Eat What You Are: A Study of Ethnic Food Traditions* (Toronto: McClelland and Stewart, 1979), p. vii (insert mine).
40. These ways culture manifests itself in the world are usually referred to as the artistic, humanistic, historical, anthropological, ecological, and biological manifestations of culture. Detailed information on this is contained in the first four chapters of *Culture: Beacon of the Future*, cited earlier; the book was published by Adamantine Press in the UK and Praeger/Greenwood in the United States in their *Twenty-first Century Series* in 1998.
41. Weintraub, *Visions of Culture*, pp. 117–118.
42. John Cowper Powys, *The Meaning of Culture* (New York: W. W. Norton and Company, 1929), p. 77.

43. Peter Wohlleben, *The Hidden Life of Trees: What They Feel, How They Communicate* (Vancouver: Grey Stone Books and David Suzuki Institute, 2015), p. 3.
44. Alfred Kroeber and Clyde Kluckhohn, *Culture: A Critical Review of Concepts and Definitions* (New York: Vintage Books, 1952), p. 290.
45. Jin Li, *Cultural Foundations of Learning: East and West* (New York: Cambridge University Press, 2012), p. 8.
46. Eleanora Barbieri Masini, *The Futures of Culture*, volume 1, *Meeting of the Working Group on the Futures of Culture, 9-10, January 1990* (Paris: UNESCO, 1991), p. 6.
47. Schafer, *Revolution or Renaissance*. See Part I, chapters 1 to 4, pp. 9–118 for a detailed account of the origins, evolution, and mechanics of the economic age.
48. *Ibid.* See Part I, pp.119–135 for an assessment of the strengths and the shortcomings of the economic age.
49. Schafer, *Culture: Beacon of the Future*. See pp. 13–82 for an examination of the many different perceptions, definitions, and manifestations of culture that have been advanced throughout history, from the earlier and narrower artistic, humanistic, historical, and psychological ones to the more recent and far broader and more all-encompassing anthropological, sociological, ecological, and biological ones. When these perceptions, definitions, and manifestations are examined in depth and in totality, there is very little in the world that is not concerned with or connected to culture and cultures, especially the anthropological or holistic perception, definition, and manifestation of culture and cultures as wholes or total ways of life. Also see Kroeber and Kluckhohn, *Culture: A Critical Review of Concepts and Definitions*.

CPSIA information can be obtained
at www.ICGtesting.com
Printed in the USA
FSHW021117190121
77663FS